Someone like...
ADELE

Someone like…

ADELE

CAROLINE SANDERSON

OMNIBUS PRESS

London / New York / Paris / Sydney / Copenhagen / Berlin / Madrid / Tokyo

Cover designed by Michael Bell Design
Picture research by Jacqui Black

ISBN: 978.1.78038.308.8
Order No: OP54472

Exclusive Distributors
Music Sales Limited,
14/15 Berners Street,
London, W1T 3LJ.

Music Sales Corporation,
257 Park Avenue South,
New York, NY 10010, USA.

Macmillan Distribution Services,
56 Parkwest Drive
Derrimut, Vic 3030,
Australia.

Typeset by Phoenix Photosetting, Chatham, Kent
Printed in the EU

A catalogue record for this book is available from the British Library.

Visit Omnibus Press on the web at www.omnibuspress.com

When you were young
And on your own,
How did it feel
To be alone?

'Only Love Can Break Your Heart'
Neil Young, 1970

Contents

Prologue

Something In The Way She Sings

This is me on my knees really.

Adele on 'Someone Like You'

Tuesday February 15, 2011

It was music that took to the stage and held it that night. It didn't need to storm it with swear words or attitude. Or scripted gags. Or boozed-up pranks and ill-considered insults hurled at rivals. All it needed was someone like Adele.

In the wake of accusations that its annual awards extravaganza had become not only "tedious, embarrassing and irrelevant", but an "outdated relic", the British Phonographic Industry elected to make a few changes for 2011. Its 31st Brit Awards ceremony would move east, switching from Earls Court to the O2 Arena; a new awards trophy - a Vivienne Westwood-designed Britannia figurine draped in the Union flag - would go home with the winners; and the focus for the show would shift from the antics of celebrity presenters to live performances by the evening's most talked-about artists. "I desperately want more gravitas. I want it to be fundamentally about music," incoming Brits chairman and CEO of Universal Music UK, David Joseph told *The Guardian*.

Lined up to perform at the ceremony – to be hosted by actor and comedian James Corden – was a stellar cast consisting of the newly crowned 2011 award winners: Rihanna, Mumford & Sons, Plan B, Arcade Fire, Tinie Tempah, Cee Lo Green, Paloma Faith and Take That.

And then there was Adele, who hadn't been nominated for anything.

Take That stomped onto the stage, behind a squad of parading "TT" branded riot police.

Adele took to the stage to be met only by a pianist.

And she just sang. And she meant every word. And the effect on all those who watched was tangible.

Her bewitching voice swelled out to reach every corner of that vast venue, and silenced it. Every audience member, every celebrity guest, every music exec.

In five mesmerising minutes, Ade'   her audience of music's power to transfix those who lis   se directly with their emotions in a way that no other ı.   ıcan manage. As 'Someone Like You' came to an end, her vocal cracked with raw feeling, and she seemed to bite away tears, beset by memories of her own making.

When Adele sang, all the rest – the champagne, the rock'n'roll trappings, the choreographed strutting and posturing, even the awards themselves – fell away and evaporated into the night; sounds and furies signifying less, much less than this.

The Brits had recouped some integrity. And Adele had become a superstar. The praise for her performance was rapturous and well-nigh universal.

"A virtuoso performance by Adele of her song 'Someone Like You' entranced and enchanted the arena in equal measure," enthused *The Guardian*

"While the O2 has ample capacity for pyrotechnics and casts of thousands in Brit performances, the simplicity of Adele's song - just a flawless live vocal accompanied by piano - had guests on their feet in appreciation," reported the *BBC News* website.

"Adele stole the show at last night's Brit Awards," pronounced *The Mirror*.

"Adele knocking everyone for six with no bells and whistles, just a piano, her gorgeous voice and a monster song," raved the *Daily Telegraph*.

And it wasn't just the critics who were wowed. In the wake of her Brits performance, more than 5.5 million people watched it on YouTube. 'Someone Like You', released as a single three weeks previously, leapt to number one. With her second album, *21*, already occupying the number one spot in the album charts, Adele became the first living artist since The Beatles to achieve two Top 5 hits in both the official singles and the official album charts.

Later, Adele referred to February 15, 2011 as the "most life-changing night of my life". There had, in truth, already been other life-changing nights. Like the night she came across a CD by Etta James. The night a friend uploaded her early songs to Myspace. The night she appeared on US prime-time show *Saturday Night Live*. The night she hit a cheating boyfriend in the face. And ran.

But the night of the Brit Awards was something special. It was something in the way she sang.

Someone Like You. No-one quite like Adele.

This is her story. So far.

Chapter 1

Dreams

I taught me how to sing.

Adele, 2008

This is a story of hometown glory. It begins in North London, the postal area of N17 to be precise. Famous for its Premier League football team, Spurs, Tottenham is one of the most ethnically diverse areas of London; it is only six miles north of the glitz and bright lights bustle of the West End, but it could be a hundred miles away. Though no less a figure than Henry VIII once hunted in its long-vanished woods, the recent history of this deprived part of London is much less royal. It has the highest unemployment rate in London and one of the highest in the United Kingdom. Regarded as a hotspot for gangs and gun crime, Tottenham is also a long-standing hotbed of tensions between the African-Caribbean community and the police. In the summer of 2011, widespread rioting across the country was triggered by the fatal shooting in Tottenham of a mixed-race man by officers of the Metropolitan police.

It was in this often-troubled area of Britain's capital city that Adele Laurie Blue Adkins was born on May 5, 1988, at the North Middlesex Hospital. Her "arty" mother, Penny Adkins, was 18 years old and single. "She fell pregnant with me when she would have been applying for uni, but chose to have me instead," Adele said later. Although not named on her birth certificate, her father was Mark Evans, "a really big Welsh guy who works on the ships and stuff". Evans only figured briefly in her life as Adele was growing up, but she had her mum's extended family around her and didn't miss what she had barely known. "I had, like, 30 cousins living down the road so I'd go and see them, always arguing and hating to share, then I'd be back home to my tidy room and unbroken toys and no fighting over my Barbie. It was like I had the best of both worlds," she recalled. They were good times. "We had no money. But I had the best childhood ever." This slightly chaotic, convivial, family-orientated start in life undoubtedly contributed to her groundedness, which would be such an important part of her subsequent success.

Adele says she was obsessed with voices from the age of three, an age most of us can barely remember: "I used to listen to how the tones would change from angry to excited to joyful to upset." It was her mother who took Adele to her first gig as a small child, to see The Cure at Finsbury Park. The Cure, a post-punk band with gothic overtones, whose song lyrics tended to the dark and tormented, had built up a loyal cult following over the years. Adele would later include a haunting version of their 'Lovesong' on her second album, *21*, in tribute to those days. The gigs are Adele's earliest memories. She also recalls her mum sneaking her into a concert by The Beautiful South at Brixton Academy. "It was an amazing gig, really raucous but really fantastic," she remembered. "I was so little I couldn't see anything, but there was a bodybuilder standing near us, so my mum just put me on his shoulders, and then I could see perfectly."

And then there was an East 17 concert when she was six. Her puppy love for the Walthamstow boy-band lingered at least until she was 18, when she went to their 2006 reunion gig at Shepherd's Bush Empire. "Best gig, ever!" was Adele's verdict for *Q* magazine.

Penny – a trained masseuse, artist and furniture-maker, and something of a hippy – didn't merely expose her daughter to all kinds of music by taking her to gigs from a young age. She was also keen to encourage Adele's early singing prowess, arranging all the lamps in the house to shine a spotlight on her daughter. The scene was strangely prescient of the stage set for the 'Adele Live' tour 18 years later, with its vintage lamps and front-room feel.

Aged five, at an hour when most infants are tucked up in bed, Adele was also allowed to stand on the table at dinner parties and entertain the company with her rendition of 'Dreams', a stirring and catchy 1993 UK number one hit for Gabrielle. Brit award-winner Gabrielle was a soulful black singer-songwriter from nearby Hackney who had become Adele's first singing idol. As part of her glamorous but unconventional image, Gabrielle sported a black sequinned eye patch to disguise a drooped eyelid. It was a style statement that Adele would briefly try herself when she sang for the first time in public for a school show, performing Gabrielle's follow-up hit, 'Rise'. "Embarrassingly, my mum made me an eye patch with sequins, to look like her," she told *The Sun*. "I used to get in trouble and wear it at school and say, 'I've hurt my eye'." But she soon cast the eye patch aside when the inevitable teasing started.

Another important early influence on the young Adele was girl band the Spice Girls. "Even though some people think they're uncool, I'll never be ashamed to say I love the Spice Girls because they made me who I am," she said. "I got into music right in their prime when they were huge." Formed in 1994, the Spice Girls were a pop phenomenon, their famous nicknames – Scary, Baby, Ginger, Posh and Sporty – rendering them instantly identifiable to their impressionable young fans. Though often critically panned for being manufactured and deeply untalented musically, the group's oft-bandied slogan, 'Girl Power', with its message of empowerment, appealed to young girls and adolescents, and became a mantra for millions of them. "They're the reason I wanted to be an entertainer. Obviously they're not great singers and I knew that when I was about seven. But what they did was amazing," she remembered.

Like many other girls of her age, Adele's other early musical preferences were for the chart-topping "bubblegum" pop bands of the nineties, including East 17 and All Saints. But thanks once again to her music-loving mother, she was also exposed to a wider spectrum of musical influences than many of her peers. Penny would play music by Tom Waits, Jeff Buckley and 10,000 Maniacs, as well as The Cure.

Every bar was soaked up by the melodious young mind of Adele Laurie Blue Adkins, and it all went into the musical mix that would later make her such an appealing recording artist. Her striking openness to all kinds of music was a trait which would remain with her, as her exposure to different genres broadened.

Then, when Adele was nine, she and her mother moved to Brighton. Penny thought that the arty seaside town would be a better place to pursue her own creative interests. Adele, however, hated it. "The people seemed really pretentious and posh, and there were no black people there," she told *The Times*. "I was used to being the only white kid in my class in Tottenham."

Fortunately for Adele, the move didn't work out. By the time she was 11, she and her mother had moved back to their hometown, this time to a flat in West Norwood, in South London. By this time, Penny had also met the man who was to become Adele's stepfather.

Adele's new South London friends embraced a black soul vibe, and soon had her listening to R&B and the likes of Destiny's Child, Faith Evans, Lauryn Hill, Mary J Blige and P Diddy. But, as ever, Adele was never going to be stuck listening to one type of music. She also remembers singing along, aged 11, to Tom Jones' *Reload* album, crooning into a can of Impulse body spray, and liking the effect it produced on her mother and stepfather. "They were like, bloody hell, you're a *singer*."

As Adele entered her teens, she made several more musical discoveries, all of which would have a defining impact on her future productions. Perhaps the most important was Pink, the sassy American singer-songwriter with bags of attitude and a powerhouse voice, whose name was reputedly coined in tribute to the character of Mr Pink in Quentin Tarantino's debut film, *Reservoir Dogs*. In November 2002, Adele went to Pink's gig at Brixton Academy, following the release of her second album, *M!ssundaztood*. "I had never heard… someone sing like that live. I remember sort of feeling like I was in a wind tunnel, her voice just hitting me. It was incredible," remembered Adele later.

Also at the gig that night was a reviewer from the *NME*. "Although Pink will stop at absolutely nothing to get the recognition she craves, there's a twist - she does it all on her own terms," he wrote. "Others

- the *Popstars* lot and more - will do anything they're told to do for a shot at fame. But fame alone doesn't do it for Pink. Pink really wants to mean something." Perhaps it wasn't just Pink's voice which so impressed Adele. Something about the seriousness of her attitude to her music may also have rubbed off on the 14 year old that night.

For it's not too dramatic to say that a new musical philosophy was about to be born in the young Adele. It was inspired by as innocent-seeming a source as a casual browsing session in HMV. "I was trying to be cool, so I hung out in the classics section," she recalled to *The Sun*, looking back on that life-changing afternoon. "Only I wasn't really cool ... as I was pretending to be into Slipknot, Korn and Papa Roach. So there I was in my dog collar and baggy jeans and I saw this CD in the bargain bin." It was an Etta James album, and Adele only bought it because she wanted to show her hairdresser the picture so she could have her hair the same. But she loved the attitude of James' face too. "You wouldn't want to mess with her, she was so fucking fierce."

"Then one day I was clearing out my room and I found [the CD] and put it on. When I heard the song 'Fool That I Am', everything changed for me. I never wanted to be a singer until I heard that."

Etta James, an American R&B singer now in her 70s, is probably best known for her version of Muddy Waters' 1954 hit, 'I Just Want To Make Love To You', which featured in a TV commercial for Diet Coke. Written by Willie Dixon, it has been covered by many artists, among them The Rolling Stones, whose version appeared on their first UK LP released in 1964. But it was James' affecting, bluesy voice for which a captivated Adele fell, hook, line and sinker. "Initially... I loved the way she looked... the big kind of white-woman weave and her beautiful, catty eyes!" she told *Blues & Soul* magazine. "But then, once I actually listened to her... I found that her delivery was just so sincere that she really could convince me she was singing directly to me. Which is something I've never ever found in any other artist." Or, as she put it to *Rolling Stone*, Etta James' voice "took over my mind and body".

Add in the purity of tone and extraordinary vocal range of jazz legend Ella Fitzgerald, to whom Adele also began listening around this time, and something crystallised deep within the reflective London teenager. She had found her musical heartland. "Chart music was all I ever knew. So when I listened to the Ettas and the Ellas, it sounds so cheesy, but it was like an awakening," she recalled. "I was like, oh, right, some people have proper longevity and are legends. I was so inspired that as a 15 year old I was listening to music that had been made in the forties. The idea that people might look back to my music in 50 years' time was a real spur."

'Fool That I Am' was to become one of Adele's most regularly performed cover versions, and was selected for the B-side for her first single, 'Hometown Glory'. When introducing it at gigs, she is wont to refer to it as "my favourite song ever".

From then on, although sell-out concerts were a few years off yet, Adele began to galvanise her musical ambitions, encouraged by a friend of her mother, an "amazing Faith Evans-type singer" who told Adele that she had talent and should pursue her singing. After that, "everything kind of all fell into place". Adele took up playing the guitar, and went on to learn the bass and a little piano.

Despite regular Destiny's Child sing-offs in the playground, Adele was becoming restless at her South London comprehensive school. As she said to *The Times*: "They didn't really encourage me. They didn't really encourage anybody. I knew I wanted to do music, but even when I was in Year Seven and wanted to be a heart surgeon [her 'grampy' having died of heart disease] they didn't encourage that either. It was just, 'Try and finish school and don't get pregnant.'"

So Adele applied to the BRIT School in nearby Croydon, after waving goodbye to a few lingering wannabe-Spice Girl ambitions. "I wanted to go to Sylvia Young [a central London theatre school] because Emma Bunton [Baby Spice] went there," she told Q. "But my mum couldn't afford it. I was bitter and twisted." Established for students aged between 14 and 19, the BRIT School is Britain's only free performing arts and technology school. State-funded, it specialises in educational and vocational training, both in the performing arts and media, and in the art, design and technologies that surround musical performance and recording. Adele attended the open day and was shown around by a student called Beverley Tawiah. "She really encouraged me and she was a brilliant singer. I thought, 'That's it, I'm coming here.'" In a curious synergy of fates, Tawiah was later to join the band belonging to future Adele producer Mark Ronson.

Adele was accepted at the BRIT School in 2003. Speaking to *The Guardian*, she recalls it as "a school full of kids that will dance at a freezing-cold town hall barefoot for eight hours solid. And, whereas before I was going to a school with bums and kids that were rude and wanted to grow up and mug people, it was really inspiring to wake up every day to go to school with kids that actually wanted to be productive at something and wanted to be somebody." Around the time she started at the BRIT School, the school canteen regularly resounded to the songs of a former pupil who had just released her first album, entitled *Frank*.

Amy Winehouse was not the only ex-BRIT student to have found a wide audience. Though the school is careful to point out on its website that it is not a stage or fame school, its roster of successful former alumni is impressive, even laying aside the name of one Adele Laurie Blue Adkins. Leona Lewis, Katie Melua and Kate Nash all went through it, along with more recent graduates Katy B and Joe Worricker. Not that Adele remembers all of her contemporaries, despite having been a gregarious student. "That Leona Lewis must've been a quiet horse as I can't remember her at all. And I knew everyone there," she told *The Sun* in 2008. "I loved it there, it's such a great place and the support you get is amazing. Some of the shows they put on are amazing – better than any of the shows on in town at the moment."

Not that Adele was always starry-eyed about the so-called talent on display around her. "Some of the people there are atrocious, really bad," she recalled. "They all wanna be fucking soul singers! I'm all up for people who are in development, but not people who are in there for four years and start when they're shit and leave when they're even worse."

Adele clearly believed that there was very little that the BRIT School could teach her about singing in any case. "Nobody at the BRIT School taught me how to sing," she said later. "*I* taught me how to sing listening to Etta James at home. What they taught me was how the business works."

But she almost blew it. Adele was nearly kicked out of the BRIT School for her inability to get herself up in the mornings. "I'd turn up to school four hours later. I was sleeping. I wasn't bunking. I just couldn't wake up," she said. The turning point was a planned trip to perform at a festival in Devon for some of the school's most promising students. Adele overslept and missed it. "My heart exploded in my chest. It was pretty horrible. I almost did get kicked out of school for that."

Despite her near-expulsion, plus the distractions of the kids "doing pirouettes in the fucking hallway", Adele – her head screwed tightly back on – used her time at the BRIT School to get to grips with the practical side of the music industry: learning to use a recording studio, familiarising herself with contracts and budgets, and reading *Music Week*, the industry's trade magazine. It was clear that, in business at any rate, she wasn't planning on being anybody's fool. "Most artists haven't got a clue," she later told *The Times*. "They get me to sign contracts now and it's a big joke, it's like, 'Do you understand this long word written down here, Adele?' And I'm like: 'Yes, I do actually. It means you're trying to rip me off.'"

Adele's determination to control her own future career also gave her the desire to spread her wings creatively. She learned to play piano, clarinet and guitar. And, after years of singing the songs of others, Adele began to write her own. The very first she wrote, aged 18, was 'Hometown Glory', a stirring tribute to the great city that had nurtured her musical ambitions in the first place. One of Adele's neighbours in West Norwood at the time was Shingai Shoniwa, now lead singer with The Noisettes, a snarly blues–punk band, renowned for its explosive live shows. "I heard her playing this shrieky saxophone," recalls Shoniwa.

"We lived right next door to each other on top of the Co-op – that place should have two blue plaques! Awesome days: she had a piano, I had a drum kit." It was in this first-floor flat that Adele was to pen much of her debut album, *19*.

Even then, Adele had few, if any, dreams of stardom. "There were some people at school who really pushed hard. You could tell they really wanted it. Adele never really had that," Ben Thomas, Adele's fellow student and now her long-term guitarist, recalled for *Rolling Stone*. "But... everyone would be completely silent and in awe when she performed." Recalling Adele's time at the BRIT School, musical director Liz Penney said that she was already a very able singer. "Her drive to be a songwriter was evident quite early on. We'd often see her outside in the corridor; writing lyrics; picking up the guitar and learning to accompany herself."

In the alumni section of its website, the BRIT School declares: "It is for this reason why it is so important to dream... Because great people can't afford to measure themselves by the visions of their peers. They must measure their standards by the quality of their own visions... what they see for themselves. Creative people create their own worlds."

As her 18th birthday and adulthood approached, Adele was beginning to do just that. Dreams can come true, as Gabrielle had promised back when Adele Laurie Blue Adkins was just a little kid. Now the stage for those dreams was set. Very soon Adele would start to reveal some of the creative wonders of her world.

Chapter 2

Bluebirds Fly Out

The way some of 'em have gone on about me you'd think I'd made Dark Side Of The Fucking Moon or something!

Adele, 2008

A dele graduated from the BRIT School in May 2006. At her 18th birthday party in a Brixton pub that same month, she stood up and sang a couple of numbers. In the audience was Nick Huggett, A&R man for XL Recordings.

At the time, it was in A&R that Adele saw her future. "I wanted to help other people sell records," she told *Rolling Stone*. It perhaps wasn't surprising that she was still thinking in practical terms about her desired musical career. At the time, she had only written three songs of her own: 'Hometown Glory', 'Daydreamer' and 'My Same'. Her friend Lyndon had posted demos of all three songs, recorded as a class project, on a nascent networking site called Myspace back in 2005. But ever since, the response had been deafening silence.

And then a singer named Lily Allen, who had also quietly posted demos of seven or eight tracks onto Myspace in late 2005, began to get noticed. By early 2006, the plays of her songs were going up and up, and Parlophone, Allen's hitherto uninterested record label, began to get excited. As word got round about the potential of the site to uncover previously unknown music talent, other record companies started to haunt it. And so it happened that Adele's demo attracted the attention of both the celebrated Island Records and respected independent label XL Recordings. XL got in touch, but, having never heard of them, Adele initially assumed the e-mail was from "some internet perv", or at least a wind-up. In fact, as she would later learn, XL was the cutting-edge home to such distinctive artists as The White Stripes, MIA, Dizzee Rascal and Peaches, and a very happening label indeed. Not, on the face of it, the obvious home for a graduate of the BRIT School.

When he first listened to Adele's Myspace demo, which had been recommended to him by a scout, Nick Huggett was in Barcelona with Dizzee Rascal. "I just heard a really amazing voice and I thought, 'Wow, there's something special about this girl,' and went to investigate her further." Preoccupied with organising her birthday party, and planning to go to university at the Liverpool Institute of Performing Arts that autumn, Adele banged off a reply to another e-mail from Huggett. "'Can you not e-mail me please? I'm busy,'" she recalled writing. "And he went, 'I'm sorry, I just wanted to check: are you signed?' And I was like, 'Signed to what?' And he said, 'Have you got a record deal?'"

Whereupon Adele finally agreed to a meeting at XL, taking along her friend and guitarist, Ben Thomas, for moral support. Still disbelieving, she thought XL might offer her a job as an intern, but soon realised that it really was her music they were interested in. "That was when we got *fucking* excited," she later said, with typical directness.

Nick Huggett, who had founded XL as a London teenager, recommended Adele to Jonathan Dickins at September Management. Dickins has an impressive musical pedigree. His grandfather co-founded *NME*, and effectively invented the pop charts in the fifties, whilst Dickins' father is booking agent for the likes of Bob Dylan and Diana Ross. However Adele claims that the reason that she signed with him was because he made her laugh – to the extent that she had "stomach cramps the day after". The fact that he also managed her friend Jamie T, whom Adele had met on Myspace, was also a factor in Adele's decision to work with him. "I've always loved Billy Bragg and I thought [Jamie T] sounded like a street version of him. He e-mailed me to tell me he really loved 'Hometown Glory' and that was it," said Adele of their friendship.

Adele and Dickins hit it off immediately too. "I listened and threw in some ideas, and generally it just clicked," he recalled. "Signing her on was one of the most easy, uncomplicated things I've ever done." Adele mainly remembers the laughs; but, from his side, Dickins was convinced he had found a star. "From the start it was clear she had this absolutely God-given talent. It was the best voice I'd ever heard in my life." Still aged only 18, Adele signed to XL Recordings in September 2006.

Adele played a few pubs in early 2007, and then quietly toured the UK as the opening act for another Myspace musician friend, rockabilly singer-songwriter Jack Peñate, having already contributed vocals to the song 'My Yvonne' on his début album, *Matinee*. According to Peñate, he and Adele met in a club when she was 16. "We met in a very unglitzy, unshowy world and became friends through just liking each other's music on Myspace," he told the BBC. "We're incredibly close."

In turn Adele has paid tribute to Peñate for supporting her from the start. "I owe so much to Jack for this buzz," she confessed to *The Sun*. "I met Jack at one of his gigs and it was instant. We went out and didn't sleep for two days. We were wandering around Chelsea and the King's Road looking for food; it was really fun. Then he took me on tour with him and had me on his record. He's been there before anyone else."

Adele had celebrated her record deal with family and friends in the Duke of Wellington pub in London's Notting Hill. Her future was looking rosy. But in the same pub, immediately after signing, she had suffered a panic attack and "got really scared": the enormity of the creative task that she had taken on had begun to dawn on her. By February 2007, with the pressure of a first album to write, Adele still only had a repertoire of four songs. For eight months after signing her deal, she felt that she had nothing to write about. "I was overwhelmed by the deal, because it came out of nowhere," she said. "Then I met and broke up with my ex, and the songs just poured out." By June, she had written another eight.

The break-up happened because Adele found out that her boyfriend of six months had been cheating on her. "I went to the pub [where he was] and punched him in the face," she told *Rolling Stone*. "I got thrown out and as I was running away, the phrase 'chasing pavements' came to me. I sang it into my phone, went home and got three chords together." What happened to the ex? she was asked. "We're still friends. And I'm grateful – I got a multi-platinum album out of it, and he still works at a phone shop."

Despite the heartache, things were looking good musically. With an album's worth of songs safely in the bag, the month of June also brought a TV début that meant the world to Adele. From the age of four, and on throughout her childhood, Adele's mother had allowed her to stay up and watch *Later... with Jools Holland* with her on a Friday night. Currently in its 39th series, the long-running BBC2 music show – hosted by the genial former Squeeze keyboards player – began in 1992, around the time Adele started watching it. Each week it brought together studio performances by established artists with those from lesser known but breaking acts. So it was a moment of great significance for Adele when, on the strength of her demo tape, she was invited to perform on *Later...* on June 8.

Remarkably she was one of the first singers to appear on the show without actually having a record out. "When we fall for somebody, we have to have them," the show's producer Alison Howe told *The Guardian*. "She's a classic. She doesn't fit anywhere; she just has a great voice." Also guests on the same show were Paul McCartney and Björk.

Understandably, a TV début in the company of such luminaries presented a daunting prospect, and Adele was incredibly nervous. "When my mum came backstage to see me I couldn't even open my mouth," she told *The Times*. "I think she was worried I was gonna fall off my chair or faint or just fuck it up somehow."

Adele took to the stage, or rather, the studio floor. "They usually put you in the middle of the room, but for some reason they put me at the end, right in front of the audience, with Björk on my left, Paul McCartney on my right and my mum crying in front of me." She perched on her stool, guitar in hand, hair piled on her head at a jaunty angle and, despite her fears, proceeded to wow the audience with a heartfelt acoustic version of 'Daydreamer'.

"We got a performance from her that was simple, and almost naïve," said Alison Howe later. "You can see her trembling at times... You can sense her nervousness about what she was about to do, and the performance is all the better for it."

Adele continued to gig throughout the summer and early autumn of 2007, supporting the likes of Jack Peñate and the folky hippy Texan-born artist Devendra Banhart. And she continued to attract critical attention. In May she had performed in the Red Roaster Café in Brighton as part of the Great Escape Festival, inspiring one reviewer to write memorably of her that "when she opens her gob, bluebirds fly out".

Later that summer, she played a well-received set at the Glastonbury Festival. In September, *The Guardian* ran a piece by Paul Lester tipping Adele for greatness, under the headline, 'Watch Out Amy Winehouse!'. With an innocent flippancy that turns macabre in the light of what we now know, Lester wrote, "The way things are going with Amy Winehouse, we're going to have to line up another indie/nu-soul/jazz chanteuse in the wings. Just in case, like. Because you never know when your favourite messed-up Mercury Prize loser is going to succumb to the excesses of fame and OD on tattoo ink."

On October 22, Adele's début single, 'Hometown Glory', was released as a limited edition 7-inch single on Jamie T's 'Pacemaker' label. On the B-side was Adele's "favourite song ever": Etta James' 1961 number, 'Fool That I Am'. The cover of the single featured a portrait of a wistful-looking Adele at a café table. On this initial release, it failed to make any impact on the charts. Nevertheless, word about Adele's remarkable talent was still cooking up nicely. "The expectations around this single from our point of view were not huge, although we obviously think it's a great bit of music," Jonathan Dickins told *Music Week*. "It's amazing how well it's done in terms of being picked up by press and radio."

A couple of days after the release of 'Hometown Glory', Adele made a guest appearance as part of a one-off set performed by producer Mark Ronson at London's Roundhouse on the opening night of the BBC Electric Proms 2007. Backed by the mighty sound of the BBC Concert Orchestra, Adele's fellow guests included Terry Hall, Sean Lennon and Ricky Wilson. Adele delivered her first live performance of 'Cold

Shoulder', the song which Ronson had produced for her forthcoming album. And again, it brought her plaudits. "It wasn't stellar performances by The Charlatans' Tim Burgess nor the Kaiser Chiefs' Ricky Wilson everyone was talking about. Neither were the no-shows of Amy Winehouse and Lily Allen the top subject for post-gig discussion. The news was a little-known soul singer called Adele," wrote Elisa Bray of *The Independent*.

On November 22, Adele appeared at the Union Chapel in Islington alongside headline act, Will Young, as part of the Little Noise sessions, an annual series of acoustic gigs in aid of charity Mencap. It must have been quite a moment for Adele to share a bill with the man she once dubbed her first love. "I was obsessed with him. I got chucked out of school for a week for having a fight with Gareth Gates fans. He doesn't believe me at all that I love him so much." Little did she know, but it would only be a few short months before she again shared the stage with the one-time object of her affections and next time it would be in much more glamorous circumstances.

A fortnight later on December 7, Adele was on TV again, performing on BBC1's *Friday Night With Jonathan Ross* t the time, Ross was pulling in over 3.5 million viewers, and the line-up for this particular show – Jerry Seinfeld, Renée Zellweger, Jeremy Clarkson and *Little Britain* stars David Walliams and Matt Lucas – assured Adele of a substantial audience for her understated but affecting rendition of 'Chasing Pavements'. Two days later, she was back on the Beeb again, performing at a BBC Radio 2 Music Club gig in Shepherds Bush, West London. It was an appropriate choice, since Richard Russell, the founder of XL Recordings, had just been quoted as saying that Adele was "the first artist we've ever had playlisted on Radio 2".

The following day, it was announced that Adele had won the inaugural Critics' Choice Award, as part of the 2008 Brits. Fortuitously, this new award was aimed at talented artists who had yet to release an album. Chosen by a panel of 50 music writers, Adele topped the vote ahead of Duffy, and Foals. The idea of the early announcement, a full two months before the main Brit Awards ceremony, was to focus attention on the winner. And it worked. If there was anyone left who hadn't yet clocked Adele's rising star, they quickly sat up and did so. Adele wasn't letting it go to her head, however. In an interview published at the end of December she told *The Times* that the Brit Award was great, but also "really weird – I just hope it doesn't peak too soon. It's encouraging that everything's going so well, but obviously I haven't actually released the record yet, so it's all a bit ridiculous."

As 2008 dawned, 2007's steadily quickening flow of recognition turned into a raging torrent. On New Year's Eve, the celebrated, celebrity-obsessed US blogger Perez Hilton talked Adele up on his website, starting a Stateside buzz that was big enough to rewrite her schedule for the coming months. "It's frightening how in control he is," said a somewhat stunned Adele to *Time Out*. "The industry over there knew about me but none of the public did. But because he put my name on his site, I've got to go over now. I wasn't supposed to be going until May."

The New Year began with another bang in the first week of January when Adele came top in the BBC's annual 'Sound of...' poll, which tips the promising acts it believes are most likely to hit the big time in the coming year. Adele headed the list – voted upon by almost 150 UK music critics, editors and broadcasters – ahead of Welsh singer Duffy (again) and Manchester garage pop duo, The Ting Tings. "The first thing that ensnares listeners is the piercingly poignant singing voice, dripping with soul, which goes on jazzy excursions as it swings between being sultry and joyful," reported the BBC website of her selection. Paul Rees, then editor of *Q,* commented that it was refreshing to hear something different after being inundated with "identikit bands who want to sound like The Libertines". Adele, he said, had a voice that could "stop traffic".

All in all, it was an auspicious climate for the release of Adele's second UK single, 'Chasing Pavements', on January 14. The B-side featured Adele's jaunty and jazzy live acoustic cover of Sam Cooke's 'That's It, I Quit, I'm Movin' On'. The media coverage and the award nominations worked some magic: 'Chasing Pavements' reached number two in the UK charts and stayed there for four weeks, remaining in the Top 40 for 14 weeks after its release. US rapper and producer Kanye West uploaded the rather bizarre car-crash-themed video for 'Chasing Pavements' onto his personal blog with the caption: "This shit is dope!"

The newly chosen Brits Critics' Choice was also asked to perform 'Chasing Pavements' at the Brit Awards Nominations Launch at the Camden Roundhouse in London. Her performance was spellbinding. After she had finished, she responded to the tumultuous applause by making a peace sign and mouthing the words, "That was awful." Later, speaking to *The Observer*, she cringed: "I can't believe I did a peace sign on TV – like Ringo Starr!" It hadn't mattered one bit in the eyes of her interviewer, seduced like many others by a voice "so vast, pure and deep-soul powerful it could turn the very tides, the kind of voice we used to hear before reality TV invented yodelling like Mariah [Carey] as the pop kids' definition of singing."

But despite all the adulation, Adele had reservations about being thrust so dramatically into the spotlight. "I feel like I'm being shoved down everyone's throat. My worst fear my music won't connect with the public."

To camera she put on a show of do. In an interview with BBC6 Music on the night of the Brits laun she scoffed at the idea that she might have turned down the aw so that it wouldn't increase the pressure on her. "Nah. I'm an opportunist," she declared, giving one of her trademark deep cackles. "Course I'm not going to turn it down." The interviewer suggested the award might have been invented just for her. "I don't think it was invented just for me. But that would be really funny if it was, oh my gosh!" she replied. But she did admit that it was "a bit weird to get a Brit Award before you've done anything".

In reality, Adele was on the brink of doing something rather spectacular. On January 28 came the long-awaited UK release of her début album, *19*. It went straight in at number one in the UK album charts. Her worst fear – that her music wouldn't connect – seemed to be completely unfounded.

Ironically, for an artist who had been crowned the Critics' Choice, the critical reception to *19* was more mixed. A fierce debate broke out about the extent to which the hype was justified. *The Observer* thought *19* was an "outstanding début", dubbing Adele "very Joni Mitchell of N17". Other critics were less impressed. Though acknowledging Adele's promise, they questioned what they saw as the disproportionate hype around a singer whose talent was far from proven by her début album. The Critic's Choice award was starting to look like something of a poisoned chalice, with the carping having begun even before the album was released. Adele, went the prevailing wisdom, was being set up for a fall.

In his two-star review of *19*, *The Guardian*'s Dorian Lynskey remarked that its release seemed "less like a launch and more like a coronation". He felt that there was "scant emotional heft behind Adele's prodigiously rich voice" and "little bite to her songwriting".

Andy Gill of *The Independent* wrote that Adele was a classic example of how the iTunes/Myspace revolution had "speeded up the pop process to such an extent that a new act barely has time to draw breath before being acclaimed in ever-growing hyperbole and seeing their début album go straight to number one". The album, he wrote, was a "passably decent début" which "could have been so much more by being so much less anticipated".

Influential music weekly *NME* also seemed determined to rain on Adele's parade. It gave *19* 5 out of 10, and remarked that there was "precious little on the album that prevents it from collapsing under the weight of its own expectation. BBC online reviewer Chris Long was kinder. He called *19* "a genuinely touching, maturely considered and brilliantly sung opus that belies her titular age". But he too questioned the number of accolades heaped upon her when "her voice lacks a little soul and her songwriting a little depth".

To an extent, the disparaging reviews were the result of the timing of her rise to prominence. Adele was bearing the brunt of a Myspace backlash. Ever since a Sheffield band called The Arctic Monkeys had burst onto the scene in September 2005, with the fastest-selling début album in UK chart history, the emerging power of the internet to break bands by fan power had been under the spotlight. The traditional slow-burn road to stardom was being overturned. For music aficionados, it was a development they regarded with not a little suspicion. Despite general grudging recognition that Adele was the possessor of a "prodigiously rich voice", an attitude of 'the faster she rises, the harder she'll fall' seemed to lurk behind the prevailing critical view of *19*.

Adele might have had problems convincing the critics to take her seriously. But with *19* notching up big sales, you could say that she had proved herself to the public, despite those individuals who were going online to sneer about her success, bitch about her weight, and lambast her for ripping off Amy Winehouse. Luckily, Adele had already developed a robust attitude to her critics. "I read them at the beginning,"she confessed. "But then there were a few nasty ones and I thought: I'm not going to bother with them any more. I don't mind them that much, though. It's normal, innit? I go on YouTube and leave nasty things on there. If I was a really nice person and was, like, 'Let's just live in harmony', I'd be upset. But I can be a bitch as well."

And there were still enough glowing reviews to give her room a whole new layer of souvenir wallpaper if she so wished. "Bluesy like it's no one's business yet voluptuously funky in a contemporary way, Adele rocks out *19* with a unique voice and gritty sound that dazzle endlessly," said allmusic.com, adding the immortal line: "Adele is simply too magical to compare her to anyone."

It was nice of them to say so, but actually, Adele was constantly being compared with just about everyone. Not least Amy Winehouse. The fact that both singers had their roots in South London, had both attended the BRIT School, and worked with Mark Ronson had a lot to do with it. In November 2007, *The Guardian* chose to headline an interview with Adele with 'Move over Amy'. The article quoted James McMahon of *NME* as saying that Adele had "split the office. Some… see her as being coffee-table, a bit bland. But I remember them saying that about Amy Winehouse two years ago."

Adele pronounced herself flattered by the comparisons with a singer she admired. "I keep getting called 'the new Amy Winehouse' and things like that," she said. "It doesn't bother me, I'm the biggest Amy fan there is." Her only concern, she said, was that people might start thinking she was copying Amy. "When people hear more of my music they'll realise we're not alike. I haven't made a Motown record like *Back To Black*, I've made a modern pop album."

Adele also steered deftly round comparisons with another fellow BRIT student, Kate Nash. "When I got signed the industry was looking for a new Lily Allen, not the new Amy Winehouse," she said to *Time Out*. "For a while, when Kate Nash took off, the press was even saying that I was the new Kate Nash, until they heard my first single and they were like, 'Sorry, it's actually Amy Winehouse you're like.'"

Adele was also frequently being mentioned in the same breath as Duffy, the singer she had pipped both to the Critics' Choice Brit Award and the BBC's 'sound of...' accolade. Of the comparisons, Adele remarked, "I think Duffy's wicked and I think there's room for everyone." *The Guardian* music blog, however, couldn't resist posing the question, "Who's Better: Duffy or Adele?"

With Duffy's debut album, *Rockferry*, having been released in the UK hot on the heels of *19*, the press seemed determined to turn the two singers into arch rivals. "I read how we had a big fight down the toilets of some club, and we'd never even met each other!" said Adele. "When we did, it was literally like two sisters meeting – we knew everything about each other because of what the papers said."

At least website Pop Justice made the Adele/Duffy comparisons into something of a joke with a tongue-in-cheek rundown of the two singers' qualities. Duffy scored 100% to Adele's 0% for "Welshness", which, given that Adele's father was born in Wales, seems harsh; but Adele won out in more categories, including the likelihood of her "saying anything interesting at all in her entire album campaign" (100% to 19%), and the chances of her having a "million-selling greatest hits in six years" (49% to 12%).

The music critics could harp on all they wanted about Adele's success being due to nothing more than flash-in-the-pan Myspace-age hype; Adele herself was determined to remain firmly outside any webs of hype the press chose to weave around her. "I never made any claims about my success," she told *Q*. "It's the press, all you lot. I mean, come on! The way some of them have gone on about me you'd think I'd made *Dark Side Of The Fucking Moon* or something!" Her fans, she said, were the people she really needed to pay attention to. "I've been tipped by the industry and that's flattering; but, ultimately, they're not going to buy my records or pay for tickets," she said to *Time Out*. "It's the public I need to stick by me. If I'm stupid and fuck up, they'll be, like, 'I don't care, I love her.'"

Adele's live performances were also giving the lie to the idea that she was unworthy of her speedy rise to prominence. Or that she was being unduly altered by it. Her biggest show to date, in London in late January, attracted warm praise. "The breath-taking assurance of Adele's live show at the Bloomsbury Theatre suggests that such obliviousness to the cares of previous generations might be the prerequisite for a new kind of originality," wrote *The Sunday Telegraph*. "Adkins has had the kind of attention in the past few months that could unnerve the steadiest soul. And yet she seems blithely unaffected. She strides on stage, she sings, she natters inconsequentially, as though she has been doing this all her life, as though there were no difference between the Bloomsbury Theatre and her own front room," said *The Guardian*.

The integrity of those be-cardiganed, girl-next-door live shows, with their cosy intimacy, was a quality that Adele managed to translate beautifully to her recordings. Thousands of people, most of whom had never seen her live, were deciding that Adele was the genuine article. The girl who sounded like she actually was still singing away in her own front room was rapidly becoming the soundtrack of choice in front rooms all over the country. And soon, very soon, she would be seen in front rooms all over the world.

By the beginning of February, *19* was number one in the UK album charts and well on the way to selling its first 100,000 copies. With the impending Brit Awards preying on her mind, Adele cancelled a trip to Japan where she had been scheduled to perform in some shows with Jack Peñate. "I'm not going to burn myself out," she said determinedly to *Q* magazine at the time. "I'm singing at the Brits in two weeks. I don't want to be shit."

The much-anticipated ceremony at London's Earls Court, at which Adele was to accept her award as the inaugural Critic's Choice, finally came round on February 20. The Awards were beamed around the world to an estimated TV audience of 6.1 million viewers. In an interview before the ceremony, Adele revealed that her favourite track of 2007 had been 'Bleeding Love' by fellow BRIT School graduate Leona Lewis (who gave a resounding performance of the song later in the evening). Adele was then asked what she would sing if she were doing karaoke with some friends. "'Valerie' and 'Let's Stay Together' by Al Green," she replied. "I always sing that."

Nervous though she was about performing live that night, Adele took comfort from the fact that she wouldn't be on stage for long. She was to perform in the first part of a medley of songs fronted by Mark Ronson, singing part of Coldplay's 2003 classic 'God Put A Smile Upon Your Face'. "It's not really a song you'd think I'd do. It's quite mellow," she remarked beforehand. Also to accompany Ronson was Daniel Merriweather, singing 'Stop Me', before a finale turn from Amy Winehouse with Adele's karaoke favourite, 'Valerie'. Up for the Award for Best British Male that night – a category in which Adele's friend Jamie T was also nominated – Ronson was very much the man of the moment, not only for his own music, but also his work with Winehouse on her acclaimed album *Back To Black*.

Adele had dressed for the occasion in her customary loose top, leggings, and flat shoes, but in a concession to awards ceremony glitz she also sported a pair of hired Van Cleef & Arpels diamond earrings, expensive enough to entail her being shadowed everywhere on the night by a security guard. The ceremony itself was haphazardly hosted by Sharon – and to a lesser extent – Ozzy, Kelly and Jack Osbourne. Two camp gilt thrones had been provided at the back of the stage for the family members to loll on, and Sharon paraded a succession of OTT outfits. "The gorgeous Master Will Young," as Mrs Osbourne elected to call him, came on stage to present Adele with her Critic's Choice Award. "It's so nice to be here," said Adele. "This has been going on for like, three months." She thanked her mum, who wasn't there for fear she would make Adele even more nervous, her friends and family and the critics who voted for her, as well as Jamie T and Jack Peñate.

Less than an hour later, Adele took to the stage, still trying to decide whether to sing 'God Put a Smile Upon Your Face' high, in which case she might miss the top notes, or low, which she feared might not be "wow-y" enough. In the event, she chose low, and gave an understated but sultry performance, relaxing enough to have a bit of boogie on stage. MTV called her performance "utterly charming". All in all, it was a great night, marred only by Adele's outrage at The Arctic Monkeys for ridiculing the BRIT School when collecting their award for Album of the Year. "Fucking idiots. Think they're working class – their bloody mums are art teachers, aren't they?"

A few days later, diamonds returned, and hangover dispatched, Adele was asked by Q magazine what advice she would give to the 2009 Brit Awards Critic's Choice? "I'd say, just embrace it. Have fun with it. Cos it *is* amazing. Just as long as you don't mind being hyped up like you was Pink Floyd."

"It's not as glamorous as it looks, you know," Adele had responded at the Brits nominations launch when asked if she was a fan of big glitzy awards ceremonies. Little did she know that only three years later, she would give a stunning performance at the Brit Awards that would blow the whole evening away, and eclipse every other bit of razzmatazz that the ceremony could serve up.

19: About A Boy

It's like a child's view on love.

Adele on *19*

Released in the UK on January 28, 2008, and in the US six months later, Adele's first album, *19*, was a notable début by any standards. As of September 2011, the album had been certified four-times platinum, and had accumulated worldwide sales of over four million copies. Adele's "oak-aged voice and Botticelli face" alone would have been enough to make *19* worthy of a listen. But add in the full-fat soulful integrity of her songs, laced with generous slugs of jazz, pop, funk and folk to vary the vibe, and *19* became an album coveted enough to go straight in at number one in the UK album charts, and find its way onto the playlists of thousands.

Remarkable too was the tender age of the woman who had written and recorded it, a fact to which the album's simple title bore testimony. It felt like a clever bit of minimalist marketing, but Adele hadn't attributed much significance to the title, having decided to call it *19* because she couldn't come up with anything else. Even so, its straightforwardness chimed with that of some of her own favourite album titles. "The best ones for me are *Debut* by Björk and Lauryn Hill's *Miseducation*. They're ones that everyone just knows, that don't make you think too much, and are just quite obvious."

And, however hastily conceived, the title instinctively felt right. "To me this album does very much represent my age," she told *Blues & Soul* in a revealing interview in the summer of 2008, after she had hit the ripe old age of 20. "I was only 19 years old when I was writing it, and I just kind of remember becoming a bit of a woman during that time. And I think that is definitely documented in the songs. So, while some people think I was trying to use my age as like a selling point, I really wasn't at all…When I was signed at 18, I only had three songs to my name. But yet, literally within a month of turning 19, a load more just suddenly came out of me."

Those songs came out of her because she split up with her first 'proper' boyfriend, or "rotter number one" as a *Vogue* interview quaintly dubbed him later. The pain of the break-up provided an instant catalyst for the songs she had been trying to write for months. "Even when I was little, if I got really upset I'd write it down and give a letter to my mum. Songs are just like that." Adele nursed her broken heart in the only way she knew how, and soon she had 11 songs; enough for her album.

If the songs that came pouring out of her in those few short weeks had been nothing more than adolescent outpourings over a dead teenage romance, then lovelorn teens would probably have been the only ones to buy them. And yet somehow in both her lyrics, and her performances on the album, Adele manages to show both a ripeness of heart and a maturity of thought which belie her tender age. "I hate – I'm actually offended by – literal easy lyrics that have no thought behind them and are purely written because they rhyme… I… always want my lyrics to be mature and thoughtful," she declared later. For *19*, Adele had striven to channel her emotional turmoil into songs that would reach out and touch anyone who had struggled with the anguish of a broken relationship, regardless of age.

Adele acknowledged that writing an album inspired by a break-up was not an easy thing to do emotionally. "It took a lot from me to write the album. Instead of going off and asking people to write songs for me, I kind of put my head down and tried my hardest to admit things to myself and to put it into songs. It's a break-up record from the very bottom of my soul, as cheesy as that sounds. The album genuinely did just come together very naturally and very organically." Though she remained garrulous and gregarious in person; during the writing of her songs, a very different Adele had been at work. "I will sit in my room on my own for ages. I can't be around anyone. And I'll write. That's how that atmosphere [in the songs] gets created."

It was their excited recognition of that mature quality in the young

Adele which made XL so keen to sign her. "The idea with XL has always been to work with people who are original, and Adele has this ability to connect," said the label's founder, Richard Russell. "Everybody hears it as soon as they hear her... Most of her songs are about being hurt, and she talks about it in a way that's incredibly honest."

Honest Adele's songs may be; but there is more to *19* than simple acoustic soul-bearing. Adele was determined that it would also include a taste of all the different kinds of music that she loved. Though she had already been dubbed the "heartbroken soul laureate" by *NME*, Adele made it abundantly clear that she wasn't going to be typecast as a soul singer. "I never at any stage thought, 'Ooh, I'm going to be a white soul girl!'" Reviewing *19*, the BBC Music website gratifyingly concluded that the album incorporated "something for everyone without ever pandering to a particular trend".

All but one of the 12 songs on the album – the Bob Dylan cover, 'Make You Feel My Love' – were written or co-written by Adele. 'Hometown Glory', 'Daydreamer' and 'My Same' are the first songs she ever wrote, penned when she was aged between 16 and 18. The rest were written in the wake of the break-up with 'rotter number one', and were all about that one boy.

Recorded and mixed between April and October 2007, *19* paired Adele with a trio of experienced producers. Jim Abbiss, noted for his work with The Arctic Monkeys and Kasabian, produced eight tracks. Francis 'Eg' White, who had worked with Will Young, Joss Stone and James Morrison, produced three. And then there was Mark Ronson. Brought in for a single track, he too left his distinctive mark on the album. Ronson was better known than Adele herself when they worked together, having produced Amy Winehouse's bestselling album, *Back To Black*. At the 2008 Brits ceremony where Adele received her Critic's Choice Award, Ronson had scooped the Award for Best British Male artist.

The contrasting contributions of her three very different producers helped turn the green promise of Adele's songs into a winning album, and she expressed her gratitude in the album's sleeve notes. Her thanks went to Abbiss "for capturing the moments"; to White for helping her "moan about love productively"; and to Mark 'don't fall over' Ronson for "bringing the tune to life".

Daydreamer

Appropriately for an album that would introduce a distinctive new voice, *19* opens with a folky and bright acoustic guitar track which shows off Adele's talent in its purest form. One of the first songs she ever wrote, 'Daydreamer' is a bittersweet song of yearning about a boy she was in love with, "like, proper in love with". In January 2008, Adele told *The Sun* that the boy - "still one of my best friends" - was bisexual. "I am so jealous of girls anyway that having to fight with boys as well, I just couldn't do it. But I started falling in love with him around my 18th birthday. He convinced me that it would be fine but that night he kissed one of my best boyfriends and I was like: 'Get lost!'". Adele's matter-of-fact description of what happened does not endow the incident with a great deal of romance. In fact, it resulted in some of the tabloid newspapers running mildy salacious pieces about the song, under such choice headlines as 'Adele's Bi Guy'.

In the song itself, however, the gorgeous image she romantically, briefly made of 'Bi Guy' in her mind comes across beautifully. 'Daydreamer' is about everything she wanted him to be, about the daydream of him. Instead of running away, he would be there for hours, sitting on her doorstop and looking like he'd been there for life; the man who could "change the world with his hands behind his back"; the one that she was "hoping for". Reminiscent of Lily Allen in her half-spoken, London-accented vocal for the verses, Adele also plucks out shades of Nina Simone in the chorus.

'Daydreamer' was produced by Jim Abbiss. If the aim of the album's more acoustic tracks was to let the sheer quality of Adele's voice shine forth unalloyed, he proved the ideal man for the job. In an interview with *Sound on Sound* in September 2006, he had remarked: "I loathe the way the industry has gone, with people justifying their roles as being more important than what we are all here for, which is somebody coming up with a great idea and getting that on a record. If I can help people to get their ideas coming out of a pair of speakers, so they want to race home and play it to their friends, that's what excites me."

The verdict from popmatters.com was that Abbiss' spare arrangements both on 'Daydreamer' and on 'Best For Last' had brought out Adele's voice to "peak performance". Allmusic.com praised the track as well, finding that "it engulfs the listener with a gorgeous feeling of awe and wonderment".

Best For Last

Also produced by Jim Abbiss, the retro sound of 'Best For Last' spins out a sorry tale of unrequited love. Or at least a tale of regret for those words of love you long to hear from the object of your affections, but never do.

Adele's discreet bass guitar once again gives her voice the chance to impress, but there is a little more instrumental action here. Some understated piano chords and a rolling drum beat punctuate the ride from time to time, and each chorus puts a bit more pith on the track, but everything stands well back to give ample room for Adele's haunting vocal to shine. Adding just a little weight are backing vocals from Jack Peñate, returning the favour after Adele had guested on his laid-back 2007 album track, 'My Yvonne'. 'Best For Last' also features smooth backing vocals from The Life Gospel Choir, adding a nice blast of gospel to the mix.

'Best For Last' epitomises what *19* does best. It's a subtly soulful track; unshowy, and not considered weighty enough to be released as a single. But the hoarse emotion evident in Adele's voice in its more gravelly moments beautifully conveys the depth of feeling in the lyrics. And the lovely little lean that Adele gives to the ascending notes of melody as she accompanies herself on the bass reminds us that she is an accomplished musician as well as a singer. It's an attribute that makes itself much scarcer on *21*, but one worth celebrating on this earlier outing. 'Best For Last' reminds us that Adele is as adept at acoustic purity and simplicity, as she is at getting her voice around songs on the scale of 'Rolling In The Deep'. The pull on the heartstrings from her less celebrated tracks can be just as strong.

Chasing Pavements

'Chasing Pavements' has the craziest genesis of any track on the album. Born chaotically and inauspiciously out of a heartbreaking night that marked another lowpoint in Adele's love life, it would eventually take on triumphant life as a single, and become one of the songs that would help break her in America.

Adele has been asked on numerous occasions about the origin of the song's enigmatic title. Her accounts vary a little. But the essence is this. She had a fight with the boy she was in love with, in a club in the early hours of the morning because she had discovered he was cheating on her. She punched him in the face, and was thrown out. Outside, she started to run down Oxford Street. And as she was running, the phrase 'chasing pavements' came into her mind. Despite her distressed state, the inveterate songstress in her recognised the germ of an idea. She stopped, sang the lyric into her mobile phone, went home and wrote three chords to go with them. "It's about: should I give up, or should I just keep trying to run after you when there's nothing there?" said Adele of the song that was born from these heat-of-the-moment beginnings.

Adele collaborated on the song with 'Eg' White, who had acquired something of a reputation for making hits happen. His credits included 'You Give Me Something' and 'It's A Wonderful World', penned with James Morrison, and a 2004 Ivor Novello Award for the song 'Leave Right Now', written for Will Young. Adele was keen to work with White from the beginning "because I wanted that radio song. I wanted that big kind of commercial tune to get me noticed by people. Because, while personally I'd happily still sing to 10 people in a pub like I used to, I want as many people as possible to hear my music. In that way, 'Chasing Pavements' was quite intentional, though the way the song itself came about definitely wasn't!"

Serendipitously, the night of the pavement-chasing had taken place just as Adele had begun to work with White. Despite her inner turmoil, and lack of sleep, Adele lost no time in giving him the raw material. "I went to Eg's studio the next morning with these couple of shitty chords I'd figured out earlier that same day – and then he took those two chords and a chorus and made it into 'Chasing Pavements'!" It became what Adele dubbed a "big Burt Bacharach-tinged and almost middle-of-the-road" song, with lush string arrangements.

Chosen as her second single, 'Chasing Pavements' was released in the UK on January 14, a fortnight before the album release of *19*. By January 20 it had reached number two in the singles charts on downloads alone. To accompany the song, XL released a video shot by Matthew Cullen from production company Motion Theory. The action centres on a car crash in London's Hyde Park and shows a man and a woman laid out motionless on a park pavement, following the accident. The story of their relationship is related as they roll to and fro in a series of precisely choreographed moves along the pavement which chart their break-up following the man's infidelity, and their eventual reunion. The tale is interspersed with shots of Adele singing, as she sits with an unidentified man in a parked car at the scene of the accident. Ambulance crews arrive and Adele gets out of the car to observe the action as she concludes the song which reflects on the wisdom of staying in a car crash of a relationship.

The video has a surreal, disturbing quality about it which, although in keeping with the song's strange origins, left many people mystified. In spite of the apparent ambiguity over its exact interpretation, the video later won an MTV Video Music Award for Best Choreography in September 2008.

While Adele always maintained that the phrase 'chasing pavements' had popped into her head completely randomly, things got even more surreal when it emerged that the expression she claimed to have invented already existed in gay parlance. Its connotations were various, with some more obscene than others. It led some to conclude that the song title must mean either that Adele herself was gay, or that she had a thing about pursuing gay men. The fact that she had already revealed that 'Daydreamer' was about falling in love with a bisexual friend served to stoke these rumours.

In September, the *Daily Mail* reported that 'Chasing Pavements' was causing controversy in America because of the claims that it was a gay anthem. Certain US radio stations were, it said, refusing to play the single as a consequence. But, speaking at the Nationwide Mercury

Awards, Adele said that the rumour had originated with "some weirdo on the Net".

NME called 'Chasing Pavements' "a booming shout-out from the middle of the yellow brick road to fame... liberally drenched with... showgirl chutzpah", while *The Observer* remarked that the track "starts out sounding almost like vintage Portishead before yet more soaring strings take it somewhere less icy".

'Chasing Pavements' was Adele's first single to get a global release, launching in several countries across Europe as well as the UK in January 2008, and in the US in June of that year. Although it wasn't to bring Adele a number one single in any of these places, it went on to win her a Grammy for Best Female Vocal Performance.

And, despite its less than auspicious beginnings, Adele remained fiercely proud of the song. "I thought I'd be best known for more acoustic songs like 'Hometown Glory' and 'Daydreamer'. The fact I'm famous instead for this... is a bit surprising! But... I think 'Chasing Pavements' was a great set-up. I'm very proud of that song. And I think the way people have connected with it is amazing."

Cold Shoulder

'Cold Shoulder', which tells of the dying throes of Adele's love affair, was the third single to be released from *19* in the UK, appearing in April 2008. Her wistful ballad 'Now And Then' graced the B side. 'Cold Shoulder' was written by Adele with input from songwriter and producer Sacha Skarbek. Skarbek had previously written with the likes of Duffy, Beverley Knight and James Blunt, with whom he had penned the number one hit 'You're Beautiful'. "Sacha gave me my education in the art of songcraft," Blunt once said.

'Cold Shoulder' is Adele's sole collaboration on the album with feted producer Mark Ronson, renowned for his work with artists like Amy Winehouse, Robbie Williams and Lily Allen, as well as his own Brit award-winning compilation, *Version*. On 'Cold Shoulder', Ronson hallmarks *19* with a fresh, funky beat and an upbeat groove which adds spice to Adele's mix, and peps up the pace after the essentially acoustic numbers that precede it.

It was Adele herself, not her record company, who decided that Ronson was the man to provide exactly what the track needed. "When I first played the song 'Cold Shoulder' to XL it had no beats. It was just vocals and keyboards. But, while they really liked it and thought it was charming, I was like, 'No, you're wrong! Right now my album lacks rhythm! We need something fast on it!'" And having been a fan since his 2003 album *Here Comes The Fuzz*, Adele already knew that Mark Ronson "did beats".

XL duly set up a meeting between Adele and Ronson. Ronson apparently forgot about it, and arrived very late. By the time he turned up Adele was "pissed off my face, smoking cigarettes and watching *Jerry Springer*! So it was just the most awkward meeting ever! But we ended up making a great track together". Off her face she may have been, but Ronson remembers Adele as a "very obviously teenage girl" determined to be her own woman. "She said, 'I've got this song, 'Cold Shoulder', which *you* are going to produce'. I was quite taken aback. She has a very clear vision of what she's doing."

Ex-Jamiroquai bassist Stuart Zender plays on the song, which features some groovy guitar riffs and a rolling marching-band-style drumbeat. The middle eight springs a surprise, too, as it segues into discordant Sergeant Pepper-style harmonies. The whole production is eerily reminiscent of Massive Attack's classic 1991 trip-hop track 'Unfinished Sympathy', which still regularly pops up on Best Song of All Time lists.

On the song's single release, the accompanying video featured sultry close-ups of an aggrieved but luminous Adele, wringing restless hands as she sings in a darkened room full of rapidly melting ice statues, posed in attitudes of despair.

"When Mark Ronson jolts Adele out of her comfort zone for the dramatic, sassy 'Cold Shoulder', getting her to play the wronged woman over some white hot funk percussion, the results are spectacular," commented one reviewer.

Pronouncing 'Cold Shoulder' the album's highlight, *NME* said, "With its flickering, panoramic production and – at last – an imbued sense of drama... it's a great vehicle for her totemic timbre."

The song's anguished lyrics made another reviewer positively mumsy with sympathy. "When… she sings… you feel like bringing her a saucer of HobNobs before trying to convince her that no man is worth this kind of heartache."

Crazy For You

'Crazy For You' is a warm and contained little song both about loopy infatuation, which is given into, despite one's best efforts, and desires voiced in the vain hope that they might one day be returned in kind. After the instrumental dramas of the two preceding tracks, 'Crazy For You' returns us to Adele's bare voice in another Jim Abbiss-produced track. It has much in common with his first contribution to the album: paring everything back to Adele and her guitar; but with an arpeggio picked out from the lower range of her guitar rather than high up on the bass. Spare as it is, the song packs in hints of jazz and country, as well as a gentle fifties nostalgia trip. There's surely a little nod in the direction of Patsy Cline and her 'Crazy', both in the swing of the tempo and the sorely yearning lyric.

"No one has put words and music to long, wet, workaday Tuesday afternoons of unrequited love as well as she does on 'Crazy For You'," was the cute verdict from *The Times*.

Melt My Heart To Stone

Under another enigmatic title, Adele writes of the acute, one-sided weakness of trying to hold onto a love affair that the other party has already walked away from. She wrote the track in a raw state of hurt, immediately following her break-up, and later admitted that it was a song she often found difficult to perform live because of the memories it evoked.

Even on the recorded version, produced by Eg White with a deft balance between Adele's voice and the instrumental mix, the intensity of the hurt which infused its composition lingers. There are tell-tale cracks at intervals through her otherwise soaring vocal, as if the singer-songwriter behind the bittersweet lyrics is duelling with the deep-voiced and powerful soul singer on show here, and in so many other songs.

One reviewer felt that the song's essential middle-of-the-road banality had been saved from blandness by Adele's "show-stopping vocal".

First Love

After the swelling tunes of the previous track, 'First Love' pares things back again, returning the listener to simply Adele, accompanying herself on the celeste this time on another Jim Abbiss-produced track. The lullaby tinkling of the celeste gives this quaint and understated ballad a different feel from the rest, and almost soporifically mirrors Adele's stated boredom with her first love.

The effect is like a music box, the melody on haunting repeat, with Adele almost robotically twirling the vocal as she tries to extricate herself from the tedium of a love affair, of which she – for a change – is the first to tire. Her feelings are reflected in the mechanical rhythm of the song, and the way she holds the words back and delivers them staccato style to fit it. With no chorus, it comes across like a monologue, delivered by someone measuring carefully chosen words, but who occasionally stalls due to the pang of mixed feelings.

Perhaps it is the relative lack of feeling in the lyrics, but despite its distinctive sound, 'First Love' seems to have gone down as one of the less memorable songs on the album.

Right As Rain

'Right As Rain' gets things back into the groove from the first rap on the snare, with some soulful R&B synth voices and a bit of Wurlitzer thrown in. The rebellious cynicism of the lyrics and jaunty melody do their utmost to put a positive spin on things "when you're feeling shit", as Adele has put it when introducing the song. Breaking up is hard to do, but it's easier if you feel you've done it on your own terms.

'Right As Rain' credits the largest number of co-writers on any Adele song: with input coming from Leon Michels, Jeff Silverman, Nick Movshon and Clay Holley of Brooklyn-based Truth and Soul Productions. Some reviewers discerned the influence of Ashford & Simpson on the track, although the Motown nod didn't please everyone. *NME* called the song "a textbook done-me-wrong Motown pastiche".

Despite these reservations, 'Right As Rain' feels like a kind of signature track by dint of the line: "It's better when something is wrong." It seems to encapsulate the entire record; a number one album which rose singing its heart out from the ashes of a failed love affair. Adele takes heartbreak and from it creates excitement in the bones.

Make You Feel My Love

The Bob Dylan number 'Make You Feel My Love' is Adele's only cover on *19*; and the idea to include it came from Jonathan Dickins. Dylan wrote the song for his 30th studio album, *Time Out Of Mind,* released in 1997, which was regarded by critics as a welcome return to form for Dylan, who hadn't released any original material for the previous seven years. It later won three Grammys, including Album of the Year.

When *Rolling Stone* reviewed *Time Out Of Mind* it dismissed 'Make You Feel My Love' as "a spare ballad undermined by greeting-card lyrics [that] breaks the album's spell", but the song has subsequently been covered by numerous artists, ranging from country singers such as Garth Brooks and Tricia Yearwood to the likes of Bryan Ferry, Ronan Keating and Neil Diamond. Indeed, it was first popularised by Billy Joel, who got his version of it out before Dylan's own.

Jonathan Dickins had loved the song for years. When the material for Adele's debut album was being discussed, he played it to her. Adele immediately loved it too, and went on to record a cover that is perhaps the most polished and emotionally centred of them all. One review said her rendition was "heart-stoppingly lovely". *The Observer* even felt that she "summons a passion that its croaking author could only envy".

In November 2008, the Abbiss-produced 'Make You Feel My Love' became the fifth and final single to be released from *19*. The accompanying video shows Adele high up at the window of a city-centre apartment block late at night. Inside, she checks the time on a digital bedside clock, sighs and, as she starts singing, she picks up her phone to send a text. As the song progresses, she continually glances at her phone, and rubs her arms as if cold. Finally, as she finishes singing, there is a ring from the phone, and the camera pans away from the window as she answers it. Her pared-down performance, rendered in shadowy black and white, allows the quiet pleading emotion of the song to shine forth.

Immediately following its release, 'Make You Feel My Love' peaked at number 26 in the UK charts. Over the next couple of years, the song went on to accumulate lots of TV airplay on such popular prime-time UK shows as *Waterloo Road*, *EastEnders* and *Hollyoaks*. But it was several airings during the seventh UK series of *The X Factor* in 2010, including a rendition by eventual series runner-up, Rebecca Ferguson, which really boosted the song's fortunes, sending it to a peak of number four in the UK charts. It subsequently re-entered the charts several times more during 2010 and 2011 following airplay on the *Comic Relief Telethon*, *Britain's Got Talent* and *Strictly Come Dancing*. Consequently, Adele's version of 'Make You Feel My Love' now ranks as one of the longest-running singles ever on the UK singles chart.

On August 9, 2011, the opening night of the second North American leg of her 'Adele Live' tour in Vancouver BC, Adele dedicated her performance of 'Make You Feel My Love' to Amy Winehouse, whose tragic early death had come two weeks before. It was a gesture that became a tradition at subsequent gigs, with Adele urging everyone in her audiences to hold up their phones with the lights on as she sang, "so that Amy can see them from upstairs". The spectacle of the Royal Albert Hall illuminated by thousands of waving phones while a huge turning glitterball catches and stirs their galaxy of lights is one of the highlights of her 2011 *Live At The Royal Albert Hall* DVD.

My Same

'My Same' is a simply constructed opposites-attract tale with a cool-jazz feel which verges on the rockabilly. Played by a tight three-piece, Adele gives it a jaunty scat vocal.

Produced by Jim Abbiss, the song was written when Adele was only 16 for her best friend Laura. At some point, the two fell out: "I don't even remember the reason, which means it was probably really pathetic," she later said. But while she was on tour with *19*, Adele missed Laura so much that she was moved to sort things out. "I called

Laura pretty much in tears, telling her that I wanted her to be back in my life and that I needed her."

Laura was in the audience at Adele's Royal Albert Hall concert in September 2011. When she came to sing 'My Same', Adele made her friend – dressed in a red, white and blue striped dress and red tights – stand up to be introduced. "I'm sure you can tell how different we are. She wears bright colours. I wear black," said Adele. "But she's the love of my life."

Tired

Despite the despairing fatigue conveyed by the end-of-tether lyrics, 'Tired' is quite a punchy track, and one which contrasts markedly with the soulful songs around it. In a full production by 'Eg' White, it delivers its sing-song, topsy-turvy lyric by way of another London-accented, Lily-Allenish vocal from Adele; and there's a generous slice of Britpop in there too.

Having spent her earliest formative years listening to bands like The Cure, Adele also adds an Eighties tang to the track, both via the muted staccato opening on the guitar and bass – the former asking questions to which the latter then replies – and the insistent popping of the synth which pipes chirpily in the background.

The unexpected, Coldplay-style swelling intensity of the middle eight, delivered late on by a big string section, seems to herald the emotional climax of the song, but it subsides quickly almost as soon as it arrives, to leave Adele tired and fed up with love again, but resigned to the outcome, rather than straining her heartstrings against it.

Hometown Glory

At the age of 18, Adele wrote the song she would later call 'Hometown Glory' in 10 short minutes. Though penned in only a few youthful heartbeats, it was this ingénue number on Adele's Myspace demo which really caught the attention of the record companies. "A combination of that voice with a song like 'Hometown Glory'... was incredible - it completely and utterly stood out," Jonathan Dickins recalled.

Adele's rousing anthem of love for her native city provides the final track on the album, but was the first to be released as a single – a limited edition 500-copy release on Jamie T's Pacemaker label in October 2007. "It was kind of about me and my mum not agreeing on where I should go to university," explained Adele. "Because, though at first I'd wanted to go to Liverpool, later I changed my mind and wanted to go to university in London." Adele's mum tried to put her foot down. If Adele went to Liverpool, she said, she'd learn to be less dependent on her family and to do things on her own. But Adele stuck to her London guns, and wrote 'Hometown Glory' as "a kind of protest song about cherishing the memories - whether good or bad - of your hometown."

An encounter on a drunken night out in Central London also helped inspire the patriotic lyrics. "I was really pissed, wobbling all over the place. This French woman comes up to me and goes, 'You need help, *dar-leeeng?*' And I went, 'Nah, it's my hometown, love.'"

The song has ballsy appeal for anyone who has deep pride in a place wherever it may be. "It's about London even though I don't say 'London' in it," Adele said. "It can be about anywhere."

'Hometown Glory's' simple melody was written on the guitar: "four chords pressing one string" is how Adele recalls composing it. However, the final production by Jim Abbiss brings in a stirring piano accompaniment instead, and the backing of the London Studio Orchestra.

Many reviewers pronounced the 10-minute wonder 'Hometown Glory' the best track on the album. "That piano, still, pokes at the heart, daring it to burst," wrote UK webzine *Drowned In Sound*. "Adele's speaking from her own bruised one here, her voice vibrant, cracking from word to word but affectingly so... Then, silence. No fussy fanfare of an outro to see the album out, no final flourishes to have the listener stunned senseless. They're not necessary. The past four minutes have done a perfect job of that already."

The *NME* pointed to its "killer piano riff", calling it a "sonorous, wide-eyed meditation on her native Tottenham", while *The Observer* was entranced by "the way she stretched the vowels, her wonderful soulful phrasing, the sheer unadulterated pleasure of her voice".

Out of heartbreak Adele had brought forth musical delights. Even those music critics who felt that *19* was good only in parts seemed to accept that Adele was set for stardom, with *Q* remarking presciently that "already *19* sounds like the work of a young artist dusting the mantelpiece for bigger prizes".

And what of the boy Adele wrote most of the album about? What did he think about it? "He loves it," she told *The Sun.* "He says: 'It's about me.' And I'm like, 'It's… about heartbreak, you fool!'"

The newspaper responded by "hoping a good fella might cheer her up a bit for the next album". Alas that was not to be. But Adele's romantic losses would remain her burgeoning audience's gain.

Chapter 3

Chasing Sidewalks

Yesterday we were outside… having a cigarette, and this punk-skater guy came up to me and was like, 'I fucking love you man!' And I was like, 'What? Who the fuck are you?'

Adele on US fame, 2009

Despite her dizzying successes to date – a number one album and two awards – doubts still persisted in the press about whether Adele really did have what it took. "The instant success that the hype surrounding Adele brings could work to her disadvantage," opined *The Independent* in early February 2008. "Unlike those artists who have built up success more slowly and established a loyal following over years, Adele has only a relatively newly acquired fanbase. Her album is now number one – but will she stay at the top?"

Adele's management entertained no such doubts however. With a Brit Award and a hit album in the bag, Jonathan Dickins and XL decided that the time was already right to take their new British talent across the pond, and launch an Adele assault on the US. It was a bullish decision which would eventually succeed beyond their wildest expectations. For a while however, things did not run entirely to plan.

In March 2008, Adele signed a deal for a joint venture between the mighty Columbia Records (part of Sony Music Entertainment, the second biggest record company in the world) and XL Recordings which would see *19* released in the US that coming summer. He may have been confident at the time, but later that year, Dickins revealed that he knew exactly how daunting a task lay ahead of them. Breaking artists into the US, he said, was a relatively new art to him, and not an obvious one either. "I'm learning about the US all the time – but it's a very difficult market to break." He quoted a sobering statistic: of the new artists that break through in America, 97% of them are domestic, compared to the UK where, he said, 49% of breakthrough artists are domestic and 47% international. "That gives you an idea of how hard America is."

To seal her Columbia deal, Adele embarked on a short North American tour the same month, playing sell-out gigs at smallish venues like Joe's Pub in New York on St Patrick's Day, the Hotel Café in LA and The Rivoli in Toronto. It wasn't Adele's first visit to the US. When she was 15, her dad had taken her to New York. "I remember going into the massive Virgin store in Times Square where I thought how amazing it would be to one day have a record in a record shop abroad," she would later blog in March 2011. In 2008, less than two years after signing her UK record deal, Adele threw herself into making that amazement a reality ahead of the US summer release of her debut album.

Despite her excitement at how her career was unfolding, it was clear from the off that it wasn't always going to be plain sailing across the pond, particularly for a hometown-loving London girl. She confessed her nerves about performing to Toronto paper *NOW*. "I love singing but I never really wanted to be a singer. It's hard to want to do something you think won't happen." Despite her trepidation, her early US gigs made a big impression on those who attended them. "I have just seen a star in the making, and I will not soon forget that performance," said a reviewer for *Goldmine* magazine of Adele's show at Joe's Pub, her first US gig. "I just can't stop thinking about how amazing her voice is," blogged another audience member.

Back in the UK, Adele followed her 20th birthday at the beginning of May with a gig at the Shepherds Bush Empire. Though it was a sell-out, she confessed endearingly to stage fright. "Thanks so much for coming," she gushed. "I feel like I'm going to cry I'm so scared. The tickets sold so long ago I had visions of playing to 10 people." This was no throwaway comment, endearing as it seems. No matter how many concerts she played; to audiences which were only to grow larger and more rapturous, stage fright would continue to plague Adele.

There was precious little time to indulge such fears, however. In the crowd at her Los Angeles gig a few weeks earlier had been powerful US TV music supervisor Alexandra Patsavas, who had been tipped off about the young British girl's talent by a creative licensing executive from Columbia Records. The result was that on May 22, 2008, 'Hometown Glory' was played during the double-length final episode of season four of *Grey's Anatomy*, a multi-award-winning US medical drama series, which pulled in over 18 million viewers. That boded well for the imminent US release of *19* on June 10.

By the time the *Grey's Anatomy* episode aired, Adele was already back in the US on the first leg of her 'An Evening With Adele' tour. It was a much more ambitious venture than her first, with Adele scheduled to play 15 venues across the US and Canada between mid-May and mid-June, before heading back to Europe to play five more gigs in France, Germany, Switzerland and the Netherlands. She was then to return home to play one of the Summer Series of concerts at Somerset House in London. After that, plans were already afoot for her to return to the States once again in August to play yet bigger venues.

Rolling Stone reviewed Adele's mid-June show at the Bonnaroo Music Festival in Manchester, Tennessee. "During her hour-long set, she showed off her huge, Aretha-style pipes. Most impressively, the 20-year-old seemed totally unfazed by her performance," its reviewer wrote. He reported that Adele had once again admitted to the crowd her nervousness about performing, telling the crowd she was "petrified of festivals" and hadn't thought many people would show up.

Despite all the extraordinary things that had happened to her over the past year, Adele clearly had insecurities. It was a whirlwind time; but it was also a very difficult time for a girl only just turned 20, who had barely been away from her beloved home and family before. "I'm sitting in a car park for trucks in between Minneapolis and Ann Arbor and am feeling very homesick. I miss my mum and my friends Brett and Clyde," she posted on her blog on June 4.

Adele was clearly see-sawing between homesickness, and embracing the possibilities of her new global life. A couple of weeks later she reportedly told a Brooklyn blogger that she had started apartment hunting in the Big Apple. It wasn't because she had fallen in love with the place, but more about what being so far from home would do for her creatively.

"I want to write my second album in New York. I'd live there for a bit, but I'd always come back to London," she later told the *Daily Mirror*. "I'm not that comfortable there, so it would be good to put myself in a position where I was shitting myself. I need to be in situations like that to help me write songs."

Those months in the US were a time of crazy mixed-up feelings, of huge buzz and excitement at all that was happening to her, but also of longing for her old footloose and fancy-free life as a girl about another town that she knew so well and loved so loyally. "Everything is happening so fast that I haven't really had the chance to absorb anything," she told blogcritics.org in July. "I take one day at a time, really. I'm enjoying it. Sometimes it's a bit difficult, but I wouldn't want to be doing anything else at all."

On June 10, *19* had its Stateside release. To mark the occasion, Adele appeared on long-running NBC morning programme *The Today Show*, performing 'Chasing Pavements', and changing the key word in the final line from 'pavements' to 'sidewalks'. Just in case any US viewers out there got confused about just what this strange, limey running after pavements business was all about. It was a rare concession from the resolutely British Adele. "Chasing pavements is a very English phrase that a lot of Americans don't get," she told *Blues & Soul* magazine a few weeks later. "A lot of people have even suggested I change the title to 'Chasing Sidewalks'! But I'm like, 'Fuck off! I ain't changin' for you! I'm from *London*!"

A week later, Adele performed 'Chasing Pavements' for a TV audience again, this time on *The Late Show With David Letterman*. Afterwards she was chased down the sidewalks of New York by the paparazzi and had to take refuge in a Russian vodka bar. "Four hours later I emerged," she remembered later that year. "Oh my, I was flying down Broadway, very drunk."

Despite the national TV exposure and the coast-to-coast tour (and the attention from the paps), *19* initially failed to make much impression on the US *Billboard* charts. It debuted at 56 and remained in the lower reaches of the *Billboard* 200 during the succeeding weeks. The US critical reception for *19* was generally positive, although those persistent, pesky comparisons with fellow female imports, Amy Winehouse and Duffy, appeared even more difficult to shake off across the pond. "This buzzed-about British bird hails from the Winehouse that Amy built," wrote Mikael Wood of *Entertainment Weekly*. "Adele croons lovelorn lyrics in a smoky voice much more mature than her 20 years would suggest on *19,*" he went on. "But with the exception of the delirious 'Chasing Pavements' – about a relationship that follows a rocky road to nowhere – Adele's songs aren't as sharp as Duffy's."

At times, the tour was gruelling. Adele had to share a "horrible" tour bus with "six stinky guys"; there were cockroach-infested motels; and the bus lavatory would block with toilet paper. But back in London at the end of June, an undaunted Adele was still talking confidently about making it in the US. "I actually feel it's not that hard to break America. It's just a case of you have to be there and have the stamina to keep going back and forth. Because, if… you show commitment, then everybody wants you. And I actually think the reason why a lot of people don't break America is because they can't be away from home for that long. I know that for me America is definitely going to be a slow-build situation."

But Adele's stamina and commitment for 'going back and forth' was about to be called seriously into question. A seismic event in her personal life threatened to blow all her carefully laid plans out of the water.

In July, shortly before *19* was shortlisted for the 2008 Mercury Music Prize for Album of the Year – it eventually lost out to Elbow's *The Seldom Seen Kid* – she had given a merry interview to Dina Behrman in the *Daily Mirror,* in which she held forth lustily about the kind of men who interested her. "I did the Radio 1 *Live Lounge* with Jo Whiley recently and I forgot it was live and I started saying how much I fancied Chris Moyles. Then he spent the whole week going on about how I liked him. But my type always changes. I like Chris Moyles, Colin Firth, Ryan Phillippe and Jamie Oliver. I like a good back. I like Jake Gyllenhaal's back. In that film with Jennifer Aniston, *The Good Girl,* when he's banging her, his back was so fit, even my mum was like, 'Wow!' So a good back and a sense of humour. I don't like fit boys who aren't funny. I'd prefer an ugly boy who was really funny."

Behrman's conclusion – "She's certainly on the lookout, and she knows just what she's after" – seemed reasonable. But it was off the mark: Adele had, in fact, already fallen in love. With someone 10 years her senior – a man she had met even before recording *19.* And with this older man, she embarked on what she would later call her first real relationship.

"It was the biggest deal in my entire life to date... He made me totally hungry," she later said. "He was older [and] he was successful in his own right, whereas my boyfriends before were my age and not really doing much." Her new love was also more sophisticated than any of her previous boyfriends, and he changed her outlook on life. "He got me interested in film and literature and food and wine and travelling and politics and history, and those were things I was never, ever interested in. I was interested in going clubbing and getting drunk."

After months of almost constant recording, touring and press interviews, Adele must have been exhausted. Wondering exactly what had hit her. Needing to take stock. And now, wanting just to be with her man. Scheduled to return to the US to play more dates in late August and early September, Adele decided to cancel them all. It was she said, in order to "balance her career, boyfriend and family".

Significantly, Adele's blog falls silent between late June and early August. There were a few gigs in between: Somerset House in London, Amsterdam and Berlin. There was also a crazy one at La Cigale in Paris. "It was one of the best shows ever. But after I'd finished, the audience wanted more. I'd sung *all* of my songs plus covers, so had nothing else to give. They started a riot literally. It was hilarious!" she said.

On August 5 she reappeared on her blog to record her excitement at moving into her own flat in Notting Hill, and talked of having been given a month off. It is still hard to sort out exactly what was going on during this period of Adele's life for this ever-loquacious woman went completely quiet. Perhaps the desire to be with her sophisticated lover made her want to shut out everything and everyone else. Perhaps she couldn't bear to be away from her family any longer. Perhaps she was drinking too much. Most likely the tumultuous events of the previous months had taken their toll, leaving her desperate for some time to take stock. Adele herself has given all these as explanations, but if any one is the real reason, she has kept it to herself. "I got in trouble for wasting people's time but I was desperately unhappy," is how she put it later.

It took the usually all-too-forthcoming Adele until the following year to open up to about this period in her life. In February 2009, she gave an interview to Liz Jones of the *Daily Mail*, after cancelling one originally scheduled for August 2008 at the 11th hour. Having made a four-hour trip to London to meet her, Jones was not best pleased at the time and had put the cancellation down to Adele being a flaky, hung-over teenager who wouldn't last in the business. A few months later when she finally met Adele in person, she quickly changed her mind about the singer's capacity for hard work.

Adele told Jones that at the time of the cancelled interview she had decided she wanted some proper time off. She had reportedly told her record company, publicist and manager that she didn't want any e-mails, phone calls or texts: "nothing". "It had got to the stage where friends would call, and I'd be working in Norway or somewhere, and they'd ask me to come round and I'd get annoyed that they didn't know I was abroad. So for three months I went to the pub, barbecues, saw my cousins."

A few months later, in July 2009, she offered some more details to US fashion and pop culture magazine *Nylon*: "We refer to that period as my E.L.C., my Early Life Crisis. I was drinking far too much and that was kind of the basis of my relationship with this boy. I couldn't bear to be without him, so I was like, 'Well, OK, I'll just cancel my stuff then'. Now I'm sober, I'm like, 'I can't believe I did that'. It seems so ungrateful." At about the same time she told a UK tabloid, "I was really unhappy at home and there was a lot of family issues going on... But I got better again. I stopped drinking."

Adele has always been franker than most about her alcohol intake. In the past, she has made no secret of her love of red wine: "My whole mouth goes red like I've been eating someone's arm," she once said. And in 2011, she told *Q* that she had discovered the joys of gin and blackcurrant. At times, when feeling emotional and under pressure on tour, or just plain lonely, Adele has admitted to opening a bottle of red when alone in her hotel room late at night. But on several occasions, she has also demonstrated that she has the willpower to give up drinking completely, either when ordered to do so for the sake of her voice, or, after her 'ELC', when she realised that she was about to jeopardise the most important thing that had ever happened to her. Come the night of the Brit Awards in February 2009, she was still on cranberry juice.

Perhaps her most forthcoming interview of all about this difficult period is one she gave to *Observer Music Monthly* in LA at the end of January 2009. "I try not to moan about it. But I just wasn't prepared for my success at all and I went a bit doolally for a while. I needed some time off and I wasn't really getting it, so I just tried to kind of make up excuses to be given a break. But it was really selfish and I nearly lost it all. But luckily I didn't."

Nevertheless, as that lost summer of 2008 faded into autumn, it was indeed looking more and more like Adele's assault on the US had stalled. She finally made it back across the Atlantic in early September, playing a gig at New York's Webster Hall and putting in a few TV and radio appearances. However, as one US paper put it, "The album... arrived in June and throughout the summer moved about 80,000 copies – not a shabby showing for a newcomer in this brutal state of the music industry. But that big breakthrough, the one that her level of talent deserved, wasn't happening." Breaking Adele in the US was proving as hard as the statistics suggested.

Then a month later, everything changed. For good. It was another of those extraordinary defining moments by which Adele's career seemed destined to unfold. On October 18, she was booked to perform on NBC's *Saturday Night Live*. *SNL,* as it is commonly known, is a long-running late night comedy and variety show, renowned for its satirical take on contemporary politics and culture. By October 2008, the US presidential campaign which would see Barack Obama elected to the White House the following month, was in its full and frenzied, final stages, with media coverage of the candidates at fever pitch.

Also scheduled to appear on the Emmy Award-winning show that night was Sarah Palin, the governor of Alaska and the Republican Party's first female candidate for vice-president. Palin's campaign had been dogged by controversies, relating both to her personal and public lives, although she had also won admiration in some quarters for her outspoken, gung-ho publicity-seeking style and her folksy speeches, peppered with phrases like 'You betcha!'. In the weeks leading up to her *SNL* appearance, Palin had been parodied several times on the show by comedian Tina Fey, noted for her close physical appearance to Palin. Fey's impersonations were hugely popular and quickly went viral.

Fey was also scheduled to appear on *SNL* on October 18 for her first face-to-face encounter with Palin. The consequence of this tantalising billing was that 15 million people – the show's highest audience in 14 years – tuned in to find out what the plain-speaking Palin would say next. And what fun Fey would make of her. And how Palin would react. So 15 million viewers also had the chance to see a little-known British singer called Adele perform two songs: one which went by the weird title of 'Chasing Pavements' and another called 'Cold Shoulder'.

Dressed as usual in her understated black, Adele looked demure, her fringe partly covering the striking sixties-style made-up eyes, which were also becoming a bit of a trademark. Even by her high standards she performed both songs wonderfully well. During the final chorus of 'Chasing Pavements', she once again changed the lyric to 'sidewalks', a concession that only served to charm her audience even more. And then, at the end of 'Cold Shoulder', came a burst of spontaneous and genuine cuteness as Adele did a few little bunny-hops back from the mike, acknowledged the applause with a childlike shrug, and flicked a quick thumbs up with both hands. It was if she sought to play down her performance, while coyly admitting, "That went rather well, didn't it?"

Before the show, Adele had turned away a VIP visitor to her dressing room. "Some secret-service person knocks on my door asking if Sarah Palin – Sarah *fucking* Palin! – can come into my dressing room. My make-up artist and stylists are all gay, and they hate her. So I say, 'These people don't want to meet her, and I don't really either'." After the show, however, Palin reportedly "tottered over with her secret-service people" and told Adele that she and her daughters were big fans. "She was really, really nice. But the funniest thing was that I had a huge Obama badge on my tit, and she was really short... So she had to stare right at it as she was talking to me!" Later, she told *Rolling Stone*, "I felt like a backstabber."

Though the show's political turns inevitably grabbed the main headlines, Adele's performances had boosted her standing in the musical opinion polls no end. "For two months now, I've been casually listening to Adele's album *19*," wrote a reviewer for *Entertainment Weekly* online. "But it took two powerhouse performances on... *Saturday Night Live* to make me truly appreciate this cheeky (yet quite stage-frighty) pile of cuteness. The striped dress, the cardigan, the Day-Glo nails, the fact that unlike many female pop stars these days, she appeared to have eaten in the last 24 hours – suffice it to say that now I love Adele even more."

As Palin's vice-presidential bid foundered at the polls, Adele's stateside rating soared. Jonathan Dickins described how he went to bed at midnight after her *SNL* performance, at which point *19* was number 40 on the iTunes chart. When he got up at 6 a.m. for a flight back to London it had shot up to number eight. "I thought, 'Wow, that's pretty incredible.'" By the time he had got off the plane in London and made his way home, the album had hit number one. "That was huge. Absolutely huge," he said. "*Oh my God. Wow, thank you so much. Chuffed and very stunned. I had so much fun on SNL,*" was Adele's reaction on her blog.

A week later, the album had climbed 35 places to number 11 on the *Billboard* 200. "Adele's combination of sultry vocals, her endearingly shy demeanour at the end of her performances, and the fact that she is the rare star-in-the-making who doesn't look as if she spent the summer at Victoria Beckham's starvation camp, obviously connected," said the *Richmond Times*. "So was she worthy of the prestigious musical slot on a show that attracted 15 million viewers? You betcha."

Adele's appearance on *SNL* wasn't merely a game-changer as far as her US sales were concerned. She would later describe that October night as "the most memorable and poignant" of her life. Future fervent Adele admirer Beyoncé had apparently requested an *SNL* ticket, but then couldn't come. Hollywood star Alec Baldwin turned up, however, and also actor Mark Wahlberg, aka former rap star Marky Mark. Adele remarked that he was "not really my era, but my mum loves Marky Mark, so I sent her a text, and my aunts love him too".

It was a starry night. But it was also a significant occasion as far as Adele's future creative direction was concerned. For also sitting in the *SNL* audience was legendary US record producer Rick Rubin. Co-president of Columbia Records, the luxuriantly bearded Rubin had made his name as a populariser of hip-hop in the eighties, founding Def Jam Recordings and working with the likes of The Beastie Boys, Public Enemy and LL Cool J. Since those early days, however, he had gone on to work with a strikingly varied roster of artists including Aerosmith, Slipknot, the Dixie Chicks, and the Red Hot Chili Peppers. He had also played a seminal role in revitalising the careers of both Johnny Cash and Neil Diamond, helping to bring their music back to the forefront of cool after years of being relegated to an unhip wilderness.

"I loved him from the minute I met him," was Adele's take on Rubin. "I loved him since I was 15 and [the Red Hot Chili Peppers'] *Californication* came out. I was obsessed with that record." Not surprisingly, their initial meeting on *SNL* unnerved her somewhat. "I watched [my performance] back a few months later, and when I'm singing I could see the exact moment in my eyes when I shat myself because I saw Rick Rubin's infamous head just behind the camera. I was so star-struck, but once you meet him he's so calming. It was a case of opposites attract." Her encounter with Rubin that night was to sow the seeds of a very fruitful collaboration.

A few days after the *SNL* broadcast, Adele announced plans to head back to the US early in 2009 for a new 11-date tour. After a turbulent summer, and a false start, a TV triumph. Adele's assault on America was back on.

The young Adele Laurie Blue Adkins, a star in the making. PAUL BERGEN

The early performance days. Adele on stage at the Great Escape Festival in Brighton, May 2007.

ritish red, white and blue. And a South London girl through and through. JONATHAN PROCTOR/RETNA PICTURES

A new song in the writing? London, June 2006. BEN RAYNER/CORBIS OUTLINE

A practice session al fresco, London, June 2006. BEN RAYNER/CORBIS OUTLINE

Barclaycard Mercury Prize Nominee for *19*, London,
September 2008 JMEINTERNATIONAL/REDFERNS

The newly-crowned Critics' Choice. The Brit Awards,
London, February 2008. The first of many award ceremonies.
ALESSIA PIERDOMENICO/REUTERS/CORBIS

Adele and Alicia Keyes at the Keep a Child Alive Black Ball at
the Hammerstein Ballroom, New York City, November 2008.
The two singers performed a duet of 'Hometown Glory'.
KEVIN MAZUR/WIREIMAGE

Solo Artist of the Year at the 2009 Glamour Women of the Year
Awards, London, June 2009. Note the post-Grammys styling.
JON FURNISS/WIREIMAGE

Captivating a continental audience. Adele performs on French television, Paris, March 2008. ROBIN FRANCOIS/RETNA PICTURES

Adele's Grammy double whammy, for Best New Artist and Best Female Pop Vocal Performance. The 51st Grammy Awards, Los Angeles, February 2009. ANDREW GOMBERT/EPA/CORBIS

Diva Fever. Adele onstage with Jennifer Hudson (L) and Leona Lewis (R) at the VH1 "Divas" fund-raising event, Brooklyn Academy of Music, September 2009. CHRISTOPHER POLK/GETTY IMAGES

On tour in the US, January 2009. And warming the midwinter cockles of her audience members' hearts. REX FEATURES

Chapter 4

And The Award Goes To

I miss Utterly Butterly... semi-skimmed milk... Walkers Crisps... my mum... my flat... my bed.

Adele in LA, January 2009

Back in Blighty in late October after her *Saturday Night Live* triumph, Adele was still hanging out with the stars. Straight away she had the thrill of singing a cover of 'Baby It's You', a song originally recorded by The Shirelles and The Beatles, accompanied by its composer, Burt Bacharach, as part of the BBC's 2008 Electric Proms season. According to her blog, this was an even bigger dream come true than when *19* hit number one on iTunes.

"It's all been a bit too much to take in this year, really. It's been so incredible, it feels like about five years' worth of stuff has been crammed into one," she blogged on October 27. The following week, the fifth and final single from *19,* Adele's touching version of 'Make You Feel My Love', was released in the UK, peaking – for now - at number 26 in the singles chart. Adele squeezed in an invitation to sing it on popular ITV lunchtime show *Loose Women*.

On November 11, for the second year running, she played one of Mencap Music's Little Noise sessions at London's Union Chapel, but

as the headline act this time. Guesting alongside her were Irish singer-
songwriter Damien Rice ("I'm so chuffed. I'm a huge fan!" she said),
and Aussie folk brother and sister duo, Angus and Julia Stone. In an
interview before the session, Adele revealed that she had started work
on her next album, but that it was hard going. "Even though I'm given
time to be on my own, the last thing I want to do is write a song."
The constant touring, she said, was affecting her ability to get down to
the job. "I've written about six songs. Four are really bad, just because
I'm kind of getting back into it. Two are all right." She would love,
she said, to work with someone like bluegrass singer Alison Krauss, as
well as more mainstream pop collaborators such as Beyoncé and Justin
Timberlake. "But I think that kind of record will come when I'm on
my fourth or fifth. I'm still a bit of a pop tart and that's what I want to
remain for a while."

This was but a brief UK stopover, however. These were whirlwind,
transatlantic times, and there was no chance for Adele to dwell on
her hatred of flying as the assault on America resumed. Less than a
week later, Adele was back in the US again, recording an impromptu,
pared-back session for iTunes at the Apple Store in SoHo, New York
City, and garnering approval from the crowd for dedicating the night's
performance of 'Hometown Glory' to NYC. There was also what Adele
referred to as a "surreal" live duet with Alicia Keys at the Keep a Child
Alive Black Ball at New York's Hammerstein Ballroom. At the Condé
Nast sponsored fund-raising event, peppered with stars, Adele, Justin
Timberlake, former *American Idol* finalist Chris Daughtry and Sudanese
hip-hop artist Emmanuel Jal took it in turns to perform with Keys.
When it was her go, Adele sang 'Hometown Glory', presumably again
with NYC in mind, rather than London.

Aside from her live appearances, Adele also was fast becoming a
veteran of big US TV shows. She flew to California for another prime-
time guest slot, this time on NBC's long-running *The Tonight Show
With Jay Leno*. Adele added considerable soul and not a little glamour
to a line-up consisting of Daniel Whitney, aka Larry the Cable Guy,
and US news anchor and political commentator Chris Matthews. A few
days later, she ticked off another of the US's biggest talk shows, when

she recorded *The Late Late Show with Craig Ferguson*. The Scottish-born Ferguson introduced his "sensational, soulful British" guest singing 'Chasing Pavements' with that now rather hackneyed language gag, remarking that "if she was an American like me, she would say 'Chasing Sidewalks'". The crowd-pleasing Adele accordingly changed the reference again, in the final chorus of a nicely understated version of the song, accompanied only by quiet keyboards and acoustic guitar. By the time the show went out on November 26, Adele had already returned to the UK, longing as ever to see her mum. Later the same day, she was back on her blog telling her fans, "I... had a roast with my ma and we watched *Monsters Inc*. I love that film. I'm so jet-lagged".

It might have felt glorious to be back in her hometown with time to chill, but America hadn't quite finished with Adele for the year. In early December came the almighty news that she had been nominated for four Grammy Awards. The leading music industry awards in the US, the annual Grammys are awarded by the National Academy of Recording Arts and Sciences across all musical genres and in numerous categories. At the 51st Grammys, to be presented the following February, Adele would be in contention for Record of the Year, Song of the Year, Best Female Pop Vocal Performance – all three for 'Chasing Pavements' – and Best New Artist. Adele was stunned. Having been told she had an outside chance for a Best New Artist nomination, she'd stayed up all night, checking the web for news breaking from the Grammy committee in Los Angeles and wondering if her BRIT School contemporary Leona Lewis had been nominated too.

Then an e-mail from Perez Hilton dinged in with the news of her first nomination. When it became clear that she was up for four awards, Adele's mum, who was staying with her in her flat, ran upstairs to tell the neighbours, despite the fact that it was 4 a.m. Adele, meanwhile, burst into tears in the bathroom and stayed there for an hour. Then Jonathan Dickins came over and he was crying too. ("He was really stingy and brought round a bottle of champagne that I'd bought him for his birthday," Adele recalled to *Vogue*.) "I can't bloody believe it! So surreal, too weird, it's bonkers!" she reacted later on her blog.

A year's hard work chasing the sidewalks had paid off more than handsomely.

The following day, Adele had to contain her fizzing excitement and get back to work. It was nice work, though, recording the first ever Hub Combo session for BBC6 Music with Paul Weller at Maida Vale studios. Interviewed on stage, Adele said that she couldn't ever remember "life without Weller"; to whose music she had been introduced by her mum – who else – when she was younger. "My mum was always huge Jam fan, and I'm a huge fan." Consequently, meeting him for the first time the previous week she had felt "sick. But he was so normal. He made me a cup of tea." Weller in his turn paid tribute to Adele's "great voice" and her "realness". "What else do you want?" he concluded. During the session, the pair duetted on each other's songs, 'Chasing Pavements' and 'You Do Something To Me', followed by a delicious version of classic fifties blues number 'I Need Your Love So Bad'. Later, when asked in an interview which song by another artist he wished he'd written, Weller immediately picked 'Chasing Pavements'.

Adele's delight at her Grammy nominations was dented somewhat when a typically off-the-cuff remark before her BBC6 Music session was reported on the BBC website in such a way that made it sound as if she was not all that bothered about winning. "It would be lovely to get one," she had said, "but I don't feel like I need awards and stuff to feel good about my music."

Adele responded to the story on her blog, writing: "That's absurd, of course I want to win one!" And, a few days later, she tried to clarify things further to the *LA Times*. "What I meant is that a Grammy is like an Oscar. You win an Oscar when you give the performance of your life. I just hope that this isn't the performance of my life... I didn't mean it to sound like I was ungrateful....I would love a Grammy." Perhaps her ambiguous remarks were prompted by her worries that her swift rise to prominence in the US would lead to some adverse critical reception stateside, just as it had earlier in the year at home.

Nevertheless, she couldn't deny that 2008 had been an astounding year. Adele, in big, baggy cardigan, rounded it off in some style just before Christmas with a cosy gig full of seasonal cheer on the tinsel-bedecked stage of London's Roundhouse. "The cup of tea that Adele clutched at the beginning of tonight's set was an appropriate symbol for the kind of intimate homecoming performance she delivered warmly to a delighted Camden Roundhouse audience. And the roadie dressed as an elf who brought the tea to her... was an indication of the show's plentiful festive goodwill," wrote one reviewer later. Even after all that had happened to her over the past 12 months though – the US TV appearances, the number one album, the award nominations – stage fright once again reared its ugly head. "I can't talk yet, I'm still nervous," she said after singing 'Best For Last'. But it was a good night, and unlike so many that year, one that took place on her home soil.

By December 25, Adele was in full wind-down mode, spending a quiet Christmas with her family. "Crimbo Ho, Ho, Ho" she blogged merrily on Boxing Day. "Ah Christmas! I was asleep for most of it, then on BlackBerry Messenger for the rest of it!" New Year was a "letdown. However, I came home and played *Mario Kart* and watched *Walk The Line* after. A lot of fun!" Perhaps she also tuned into BBC2 and settled back to watch herself on TV, having pre-recorded 'Chasing Pavements' and a cover of 'I Just Want To Make Love To You' for Jools Holland's annual New Year's Eve *Hootenanny* on BBC2.

Adele's reluctance to party her way into 2009 may have had something to do with the fact that she had given up drinking on Boxing Day. There was also the knowledge that she was due back in the US within the fortnight to fulfil her rescheduled North American tour, the one she had cancelled due to her 'Early Life Crisis' the previous summer. It would take her to 11 cities in 16 days. The awesome prospect of starting work on her second album in the months ahead also loomed large.

Adele's first round of concerts for 2009 kicked off in Somerville, Massachusetts. On a freezing mid-January night, she opened with 'Cold Shoulder' and then warmed the audience's heart cockles by performing "with such sincerity... that it felt like she was singing only to you", according to one reviewer. The cold terror of performing live remained a constant hovering spectre during those winter weeks, however. When she walked out on stage, Adele would often appear alarmingly tense, her shoulders down, greeting the audience more often than not with an awkward wave and appearing embarrassed by the welcome shown by her sell-out crowds. Once into her set however, the assured Adele would take over, and, invariably, her audiences would go home wowed.

Over the following two weeks, she worked her way across the mid-West and down the Pacific coast, blogging from Seattle on January 26: "My tour's nearly over, it's been amazing so far, had a lot of jokes and a lot of Coca-Colas!" Though still not of drinking age in the US, the temptation to crack open something stronger must have been overwhelming when Adele learned halfway through her tour that she had been nominated for three awards at the 2009 Brits, including Best British Female. Once again, she found herself vying with Duffy for all three of them.

The tour finale at the end of January was a gig at the Art Deco Wiltern Theater in Los Angeles. Adele's Grammy nominations had ensured brisk business: originally scheduled for a much smaller venue, $25 tickets for the Wiltern gig were being offered for more than $250 online. "Convincing in making one believe she has many different avenues to take on a second record," was a *Variety* reviewer's encouraging verdict on Adele's final LA gig. One unlikely guest at the show was Slash, former lead guitarist with Guns N' Roses, who turned up in a stretch Hummer and told Adele he was a "huge fan".

The following day, a tired looking Adele gave an interview to *Observer Music Monthly*, filmed in her LA hotel room between fags on the balcony. "I'm ready to go home now," she admitted. "I've just got one more week, and then I get to go home." Secretly, Adele was also overwhelmed by the prospect of the forthcoming Grammys extravaganza. She tried to pull out of performing at a Grammy-week MusiCares charity gala dinner and concert in honour of Neil Diamond. She had been asked to sing Diamond's 'Cracklin' Rosie', but she didn't know the song and didn't feel up to learning it. "It's a baritone ballad, which is just useless for me." she said. "I just like pooed myself."

In the event, she went ahead with the performance, but it turned out to be memorable for all the wrong reasons. One of Adele's ghetto nails had come off the night before, and ripped her real thumbnail. When it started bleeding again just before she went on stage at the MusiCares gala, Adele – unable to find a bandage for it at such short notice – shoved a tampon on it in desperation. "I had to go on stage in my coat because all my dresses were in the dry cleaner, so I looked like I didn't even want to be there," she recalled. "I meant to put my good hand at the tip of the mike stand, which I always cling onto, but forgot because I was so stressed." The tampon ended up transfixing the starry audience. Afterwards, Anthony Kiedis of the Red Hot Chili Peppers came up to say nice things about her performance, but admitted that the tampon had been right in front of her face. Neil Diamond, meanwhile, later apologised for stressing her out so much. "He was really, really lovely," Adele told CBS Arts Online.

The 51st Grammy Awards took place on February 8 at the Staples Center in Los Angeles. The starry line-up of performers on the night included U2, Stevie Wonder, Jay-Z, Coldplay, Paul McCartney, Radiohead and Smokey Robinson. With some of the results of the dozens of Grammy award categories announced before the main ceremony got underway to reveal the winners in the major categories, Adele already knew beforehand that she had won Best Female Pop Vocal Performance. Spotting Duffy on the red carpet, coming towards her "like a blonde blur", the pair "just screamed at each other". Duffy had just discovered that she had won Best Pop Vocal Album for *Rockferry*. The two British girls stood excitedly high-fiving each other. "Everyone was like, 'Who the hell are they?'", Adele told Radio 1 later. Far from being the rival she was often painted to be, Duffy was, Adele said, "a little bit of home on what was the most surreal day ever". Again she was nervous, knowing that she had to go on stage and sing 'Chasing Pavements' during the course of the evening. She pulled it off of course, despite being joined rather unnecessarily half way through by US country singer Jennifer Nettles, who looked and sounded something of an irrelevance next to the majestic Adele. "When she performs, standing shoeless on the darkened stage of the Staples Center, she looks oddly vulnerable and fragile – until her achingly powerful voice swirls and eddies through that vast space, revealing the force that roils within her," wrote Hamish Bowles of US *Vogue* of Adele's performance that night.

For Adele, the Awards were like an "out of body experience". "I was literally hovering above myself laughing," she said, with typical, endearing overstatement. "I felt so out of place. I thought someone was going to come and tell me off for being there." "I didn't expect to win anything. I was sitting between Coldplay and U2 at the front." Coldplay represented another bit of home for the overwhelmed Adele. "I felt like Duffy was my sister. I felt like Coldplay were my brothers, or my uncles or something," she said later. "When they called my name out, I was expecting to be asked to move to the back."

She had won Best New Artist, one of the biggest awards of the night. It was a huge shock. "Thank you so much, I'm going to cry," she trembled as she accepted the award from avowed fan Kanye West, and fellow British singer Estelle. "I want to thank Jonathan, my manager. And my mum – she's in London... Everyone at Columbia... Everyone at XL... Duffy I love you, I think you're amazing. Jonas Brothers [who were also nominated] I love you as well... All of my friends... All of my family. Thank you everyone." As acceptance speeches go, it was charmingly rambly. On the way back down, she nearly walked straight into one of those surrogate uncles – Chris Martin of Coldplay.

In an interview after the show, Adele admitted that she hadn't wanted her mum to come in case she lost. "I called her afterwards and she was crying her eyes out." Her mum had stayed the night at Adele's flat, she said, "so she could smell me". However, Adele failed to get a complete thumbs-up from her mum for her triumphant moment. "I was so convinced that the Jonas Brothers or Duffy were going to win, I wasn't prepared at all... I had chewing gum in my mouth." Gum she promptly almost swallowed in shock when her name was announced. "When I came off stage and rang my mum to tell her, she was like, 'Yeah, I saw... you had gum in your mouth!' I don't think she was impressed!" How was she planning to celebrate two Grammy wins in one night?, she was asked. "I'm going to go and put my jeans on. I like my dress but I don't like the Spanx [shapewear]... Then I'm going to have some cigarettes and just hang out with my manager and my friends."

There's something endearingly childlike about the post-show interview she recorded to camera for her blog in her dressing room, which she shared with Katy Perry. Already de-Spanxed, and back in comfy black T-shirt and chunky cardigan, with her hair down, Adele reflects on her night in breathless little snippets. "I'm very chuffed, very pleased. I nearly cried...Thank you so much to everyone... this is the icing on the cake... Whitney Houston was here tonight. Very excited, saw her on a TV screen... Didn't wear shoes all night... Saw Snoop Dogg.... Met Justin [Timberlake] but made it seem like I didn't want to meet him because I was just a bit too starstruck. And then he grabbed me in the hallway and said, 'Congratulations!'"

Although clearly very happy, there is no euphoria, no whooping celebrations at her triumph. She looks at her most animated when she mentions that she is going to get a dog in a few days' time. The impression is of a very pleased but exhausted girl who wants to go home to bed. One who still can't quite bring herself to believe she had just shared top billing with artists she had admired from afar. But one who knows that whoever might grab her in whatever glamorous location, she'll wake up the following morning and still be her. An ordinary London girl. Who misses her mum.

Though far from home, the Grammys, in many ways, represented natural musical territory for Adele. Prior to the 2009 Awards, only five female solo artists had won five awards in the space of one evening including Adele's great heroines, Lauryn Hill and Beyoncé; Amy Winehouse, whom she greatly admired despite those lingering 'compare and contrast' headlines; Norah Jones; and Alicia Keys, with whom she had so recently duetted. At the 51st Awards, Alison Krauss became the sixth female solo artist to win five, scooping the awards for her performances on her album collaboration with Robert Plant, *Raising Sand*.

Adele was already a huge fan of the album; it was "by far my favourite record of the last two or three years", she said, and it sparked an interest in bluegrass music, which was later to become a significant influence. "It just blew me away. You know when you just listen to someone so much, and you just can't really help it? So I'd be trying to write, like a Leona Lewis song, and this Alison Krauss song just comes out." she said a few months later. Another Grammy winner about to become important in Adele's future musical direction was Rick Rubin, who won Producer of the Year. And tucked away among the nominees for Best Country Performance by a Duo or Group with Vocals was a bluegrass band from Tennessee called The SteelDrivers, whose track 'If It Hadn't Been For Love' Adele was later to cover.

After the ceremony, Adele, still on the wagon, shunned the official Woodstock-themed after-party and celebrated at an In-N-Out burger bar on Venice Boulevard instead. "Maybe I should get two milkshakes. To match my Grammys," she said, laughing, to her US publicist when he offered to take her order.

When she arrived back home, she discovered a letter from Gordon Brown, Britain's beleaguered prime minister, in her piles of unread mail. He had written to congratulate her on her Grammys triumph. "With the troubles that this country's in financially, you're a light at the end of the tunnel," it read. "It was amazing! I'm fighting the credit crunch on my own!" joked Adele later. Neil Diamond dropped her a line too, exhorting her to "keep working your magic".

On February 20 she blogged excitedly that her all-time singing idol, Etta James, had been confirmed as a guest at her Hollywood Bowl concert the following June. That month, *19* had been certified Gold by the Recording Industry Association of America, and went on to sell 230,000 copies in the US during the first quarter of 2009, the fourth highest sales by an international artist for the period.

Adele had sold extremely well in the US for a UK début artist, but even after her Grammys success, and the *SNL* 'bump' to number one on the iTunes chart, *19* hadn't made it higher than number 10 on the *Billboard* album chart. And none of the singles released had made much of an impression, even 'Chasing Pavements', which Adele had been plugging almost constantly for months. There was still work to do in America.

First though, there was the 2009 Brit Awards ceremony to attend at Earls Court on February 18, co-hosted by *Gavin & Stacey* co-stars Mathew Horne and James Corden, assisted by their glamorous Antipodean side-kick for the night, Kylie Minogue, who paraded a succession of outfits. The news of Adele's three nominations; for Best Single (for 'Chasing

Pavements'); Best British Female, and Best Newcomer had come while she was on tour in the US the previous month. In the event, Adele lost out on all three Awards – to 'The Promise' by Girls Aloud in the Best Single category, and to, who else, Duffy in the other two. It was a sober contrast from her winning night at the previous year's Awards ceremony in other ways too. When asked beforehand if she was looking forward to the ceremony, Adele replied that she wasn't because she had given up drinking. "Last time I was at the Brit Awards everyone was drunk off their face before the whole room had even sat down. It was like endless Jack Daniel's."

On March 5, Adele was back in the US ready for another three weeks of gigs, this time working her way from West Coast to East, from San Diego to Cleveland, Ohio, via Texas, Atlanta and Nashville, Tennessee. Before the tour kicked off, there was a new video to film for 'Hometown Glory', in a lot at one of the big Hollywood studios. "I'm not a big fan of doing videos, but today was a bit different," Adele blogged. "I got to drive around all day on a golf cart!" What she didn't mention at the time was that she nearly ran over a world-famous rap star in the process. The story came out later in an interview with *The Sun*. "P Diddy must have been doing a fragrance advert or something. I was in the buggy with a mate and I saw him. I meant to put the brake on and go, 'Oh, you're P Diddy!' But I hit the accelerator and he had to dive out the way. As we went past I was like, 'You're P Diddy.' He just said, 'Yeah, I know.' I almost, almost killed him."

On stage, Adele was on much safer territory. Judging by the reviews of her US gigs, she wowed the crowd wherever she played. "The year is only three months old, but mark this down: a star has arrived. With little more than guileless charm, a gorgeous voice and a clutch of truly remarkable tunes, Adele delivered one of the best performances North Texas has seen in 2009," read a glowing review on regional website *DFW.com* of her Dallas concert. Such reviews must have made the gruelling 10-week tour easier, but there were other compensations too. Adele had the same tour bus driver for the whole of her US tour – a man she refers to as B – who fortuitously was from Nashville, Tennessee, and predictably mad about his country music. "On these long, long bus journeys, like 18 hours, I'd have to go and smoke up the front of the bus with him, because that's where the window was. And he'd be rocking out to all this amazing country and blues and gospel and bluegrass. I was constantly like: 'Who's this? What's this? Where's this from?'" B started making her CDs, and then radioing other drivers and promotors of venues to make compilations as well. Adele ended up with thousands of country songs on her iTunes waiting to be listened to. It was a musical education on the road, which would later prove a strong influence on her second album.

After the final date of the tour, Adele flew back to Los Angeles to appear on *Dancing With The Stars*, the US equivalent of the UK's *Strictly Come Dancing*, performing 'Chasing Pavements' while one of the competing couples danced, and applauding politely afterwards. Then, following a couple of European gigs in April, Adele was back in the US and Canada again in early May, playing Montreal, Toronto, Boston and Philadelphia, before celebrating her 21st birthday with a performance at the Roseland Ballroom in New York City on May 5, at which she was also presented with a special plaque to mark *19* going Gold in the US. Adele included two new covers in the show – 'Hiding My Heart' and 'Turpentine' – by US singer-songwriter Brandi Carlile ("I love her so much, she blows my mind, she's so good," Adele said.)

But there were to be no wild after-show birthday antics. It was early to bed to start work on an *MTV Unplugged* session the following day. In a chatty but revealing interview for CBC Arts Online while she was in Canada, Adele talked about the kind of artist she wanted to be seen as in the future. "I am a songwriter and I'm not taken seriously as a songwriter yet; not as seriously as I am as a singer. That's fine, because that will come in time... I'm on my début record. But I am a proper songwriter, and my repertoire of writing songs is broad... I can write jazz, and I can write pop, and I'm starting to learn how to arrange string arrangements and stuff. I don't want to be 50 years old and still singing 'Chasing Pavements'."

After filming a gorgeously pared back and soulful six-song acoustic session with Wired Strings for *MTV Unplugged*, Adele was finally back on home soil again by mid–May, with the luxury of a whole month off in London stretching ahead of her. She was so used to jetting around to a fiendishly packed schedule, however, that within a day she declared herself bored. While a restless Adele tried to come to terms with the fact that she was having a break, US TV viewers were able to watch her acting debut, in a cameo role in Season Three of hit comedy *Ugly Betty*.

The unlikely role came about because America Ferrera, the actress who plays lead character Betty Suarez, had been at that crucial *Saturday Night Live* show with her fiancé and had loved Adele's performance. "I met her afterwards and she was going, 'I want to get you on the show,' and I was like, 'Well yeah, thanks, but I don't see how you'd get me written in'." She thought little more of it until six months later, when the producers of the show turned up at a small US radio show Adele was playing ahead of her tour. Next thing she knew, there was a part for her.

The episode in which Adele appears centres around the screwball shenanigans at a Betty-organised planetarium event for a make-or-break assignment in which Adele has been booked to appear. When Adele hears Betty having a stand-up argument with her boyfriend, she thinks better of it and goes AWOL. Then the in-tatters event suddenly turns into an impromptu wedding when one of the characters decides to get hitched there and then. To Betty's consternation, Adele shows up again ("Oh my God, what's she doing here?") asking for the foot massage she has been promised ("Never had one before"). Later, Adele sings 'Right As Rain' on stage as the wedding guests dance around her. At one point, Betty is heard to remark: "We can't just paint stars on your ceiling and call it the Planetarium. This is Adele, not Amy Winehouse."

At the end of June, it was back to the States yet again, this time to headline at the Hollywood Bowl in Los Angeles on the 28th. This, the biggest concert of Adele's career to date, had been keenly anticipated, presenting as it did the mesmerising prospect of the double-Grammy winning 21-year-old white singer from London sharing a line-up with Etta James, the 71-year-old black American blues and soul singer, who above any other was the artist responsible for the way that Adele strove to sing. "I believe every single word, breath and note that she does," Adele had reiterated only a few weeks before to CBC Arts Online.

In the event, it wasn't to be an entirely happy occasion. Kooky US R&B artist Janelle Monáe opened the show, proclaiming mysteriously that she was "an alien from outer space". "Though she sang well and her band skirted the edges of an interesting soul-punk fusion, Monáe offered nothing of substance… to match her insufferably precious sense of style," scoffed an *LA Times* reviewer. Worse, Etta James had to pull out due to sudden illness, and was replaced by turbo-voiced 'Queen of Funk', Chaka Khan. However, Chaka Khan fared rather better than Monáe, turning in a "tidy set of durable R&B gems" which included 'I'm Every Woman' and 'Ain't Nobody'.

Then it was time for Adele. "I feel like Beyoncé or something. There's so many of you," she gasped on taking the stage of the historic 18,000 capacity venue. She chatted on in typical, girl-next-door style, telling the audience that because she had got badly sunburned by the Californian sun, she had had to layer on the make-up to the extent that she felt like a "drag queen". At one point, she phoned her mum at home in London, getting the audience to roar hello when she answered. When she ended the call, there was a delightful moment as Adele ran around the stage, looking for a place to put her mobile down.

Several times during the gig, she fluffed her lyrics, and once – during 'Melt My Heart To Stone' - she made her band – and the Hollywood Bowl Orchestra Strings – start the number again. But it didn't seem to matter much to her audience. "In a way, that charming guilelessness actually serves as a highly effective bit of stagecraft," said the *LA Times*. "Because Adele's just-folks persona prepares you for a just-folks voice, the real thing ends up sounding even more magnificent than it is." Amidst the usual *19* playlist and favourite covers, she ventured a version of 'Thriller' in tribute to Michael Jackson, who had died just days before. And she also tried out an early version of a brand-new song: a soulful number called 'Take It All'.

By July 2009, *19* had sold 2.2 million copies worldwide. Mid-month, Adele performed at the North Sea Jazz Festival in Rotterdam. It was her final outing to promote *19*, and it marked the end of more than a year of almost constant touring. Adele celebrated by getting "a bit emotional" and then "really drunk" with her manager on the balcony of her hotel. But it was time to go home. And time for 21-year-old Adele to focus on that difficult second album.

Handbags And Gladrags

I've never looked at a magazine cover and gone, 'That's what I need to look like if I'm going to succeed in life'.

Adele, 2011

Back in her early teens, Adele's clothes had been chiefly inspired by the street trends of the time. "From 12 to 13 I was a grunger. Criminal Damage jeans. Dog collars. Hoodies. We used to go to Camden all the time because we were, like, 'so dark'. Then I really got into R&B and became a rude girl – in Adidas, with a spit curl! Tiny Nike backpacks. Mine was black, with a logo bigger than the bag."

Later, before she landed her record deal, Adele saved up for three years to get her first designer handbag: a Burberry satchel. "Five hundred quid, I think it was," she recalled. That bag was the first designer item she had really coveted: a rare early concession to fashion from a girl who already cared a whole lot more about what she sounded like than any visual style statement her clothes might be making.

Five years later, that same girl had, in the space of the 12 months of 2011, graced the cover of British *Vogue* in a blue lace dress, made to order by Burberry (if you have to ask the price…); the cover of *Rolling Stone* in a black dress by BCBGMAXAZRIA; the cover of US *Cosmopolitan* in an unashamedly sexy leopard-print dress by Dolce & Gabbana; the cover of *Glamour* in a summery floral number by Jil Sander; and the cover of deeply modish quarterly *the gentlewoman* in a white-print cloque dress designed by Phoebe Philo for the house of Céline.

Adele, albeit reluctantly, had become a fashion icon, and a beautifully groomed one at that: a big, glossy, coppery mane swept back from her face, billowing down to cascade round her shoulders; apparently flawless creamy skin and huge green almond-shaped eyes, immaculately made up. And those trademark ghetto-fabulous nails, catching the eye with every movement of her expressive singer's hands.

These cover-girl days are a far cry in fashion from her early public appearances on stage. By her late teens, Adele had adopted a comfortable uniform of smocky cotton tunics and baggy cardigans over leggings and flat shoes, her long hair pulled up into jauntily angled buns, her heavy fringe partly concealing the eyes and accentuating her shyly apologetic onstage presence. As she began to be noticed by the media, Adele would occasionally embrace high fashion when she had her photo taken, and sometimes there were gifts from designers like plus-size fashion guru, Anna Scholz, who gave her a gold sixties-style coat.

But most of the time, even when awards ceremonies started beckoning, Adele was still dressing to please her comfort-loving self. At the Brit Awards in February 2008, she wore a black smock-style top with puffed sleeves, leggings and flat shoes, her only concession to glitz a pair of diamond earrings borrowed from Van Cleef & Arpels. Then as she embarked on her extensive US tour in the spring, the signature, overwhelmingly black casual wardrobe and understated make-up remained, despite numerous TV appearances, which might have put another artist under intolerable pressure to get glammed up in a style to which she was not accustomed. Adele let her voice give the show, and it did.

At the Mercury Awards that September, Adele worked a slightly different sixties look in a baby-doll-style tunic dress, trimmed with pink, and her hair loose and backcombed. She borrowed another pair of sparkly earrings, this time diamond-encrusted clip-ons worth £20,000. A nervous Adele kept touching them to check they were still there. "I'm worried I'm going to get drunk and lose my earrings," she reportedly said. "I'm used to Argos' Elizabeth Duke range myself." Even for the career-boosting appearance on *Saturday Night Live* in October in front of 15 million viewers, Adele chose not to deviate from her comfort zone: grey smocked tunic top, leggings and a black shrug-on cardigan. The dressed-down look actually won her plaudits.

Essentially, Adele wasn't much concerned with her appearance, or the impression it made. In an era obsessed with image, her attitude from the beginning was: take me as you find me, and judge me as I sound, not as I look. Quite often a press interviewer would arrive, expecting a glamorous soul starlet perhaps, and instead encounter a dressed-down Adele in jeans and without a scrap of make-up. She had no qualms about being filmed this way either: in a *Billboard* video interview in July 2008, she appears bare-faced and sporting a red knitted bobble hat.

It was an attitude completely consistent with her lack of airs and graces, and it made a favourable impression on those used to more manufactured artists. "Adele is the antithesis of the super-sleek, ultra-groomed pop stars we're used to seeing – and all the better for it," was the verdict of Dina Behrman after interviewing Adele for the *Mirror* in July 2008. "I'd say my look is shabby-chic," Adele had told her. "I just wear big jumpers over tight jeans and carry a huge bag, and that's it... I don't care about clothes, I'd rather spend my money on cigarettes and booze."

Part of the reason for regarding designer labels as irrelevant to her was that Adele had always assumed that the famous names would have nothing to offer a size 14-16 frame. It took an encounter with Anna Wintour – the formidable editor-in-chief of US *Vogue* and widely regarded as the model for the monstrously demanding Miranda Priestly in *The Devil Wears Prada* – before Adele really began to wake up to what clothes could do for her, curves and all.

Adele – despite her avowed lack of interest – agreed to do a fashion shoot for the magazine's annual Shape Issue ("Fashion for Every Figure From Size 0 to Size 20"), with celebrated portrait photographer Annie Leibovitz. Formerly chief photographer for *Rolling Stone,* Leibovitz was noted for her iconic, and sometimes controversial photographs of rock musicians, including the famous images of Bruce Springsteen used on the album sleeve of *Born in the USA* and the equally celebrated portrait of a naked John Lennon, pressed up close to a clothed Yoko Ono, shot on the day of his death. It was quite something to be photographed by her.

Not that the undaunted Adele was going to be overawed by Leibovitz, or let *Vogue* have all the say about what she wore in the four-page feature. She challenged the initial plan to put her in a tight dress. "I was like, 'I've got five bums, one extra belly. I'd rather do one that just flows over the bad parts." The shoot took place at the swanky London West Hollywood Hotel in California; but although nine hours had been blocked out in her diary, the session only took 10 minutes. In the resulting double-page spread photograph, under the headline 'Feeling Groovy', Adele lies sprawled on a hotel bed, guitar close at hand, modelling a Michael Kors evening coat in black, studded with large white polka dots.

Accompanying the photograph, which appeared in the April 2009 issue, is an interview by Hamish Bowles, something of a dandyish fashion guru himself. "There is something more period than merely old-fashioned about the way this soulful singer looks," he waxed lyrically of Adele. "She might be one of Charles II's court favourites, perhaps, or an actress painted by Reynolds or Romney, and her healthy bawdiness would certainly have been celebrated by Wycherley and Fielding."

In turn, Adele reiterated to Bowles that, "I like being comfy more than anything", citing her preferred clothes as enveloping sweaters and cardigans in luxurious fabrics, "old vintage cardies with beads and pearls sewn into flowers", leggings, and ballet pumps. Her hairdresser, Kevin Posey, declared her look was "Goldie Hawn on the Go-Go, or early nineties hip-hop – but as though Chanel had done it". Something of a mixed metaphor, but probably a suitable one for a girl who was still a devotee of high-street stores like H&M, Miss Selfridge, Topshop and Primark, despite the fact that she was now venturing occasionally into Vivienne Westwood and Aquascutum territory. And in a nod to her former Camden Market days, Adele also expressed regret that she no longer had time to hunt for retro gear in street markets.

When the largely label-oblivious London girl arrived for her final fittings for the *Vogue* shoot, she was told that Anna Wintour wanted to meet her. "It was like *The Devil Wears Prada*. Everyone was going, 'Don't talk to her unless she talks to you', and I was like, 'Fucking hell, bring on Meryl Streep'... I went in and she was so nice. She was like, 'What labels do you like?' I was trying to make up these designers that I was quite sure I had read in *Vogue* or something before." But despite Adele's lack of fashion savviness, Wintour took a liking to her, and offered her a sartorial helping hand for the forthcoming Grammys ceremony. She and Hamish Bowles settled on US designer Barbara Tfank for the job.

Inspired by the retro glamour of such style icons as Elizabeth Taylor, Tfank, a former costume designer, has made occasion dressing - including those all-important red carpet moments – her speciality. In an era when most designer frocks are made to hang on sticks, her dresses are sumptuously composed of rich fabrics in styles unapologetically aimed at flattering the hourglass silhouette of women with 'something up top'. Interesting necklines and cinched-in waists are hallmarks of a Tfank dress; Michelle Obama wore one when meeting the Queen at Buckingham Palace in 2011.

One might have expected dress-down Adele to be daunted at the prospect of being taken in hand by such fashion luminaries. But she wasn't. "I met her when she was just 20, and – aside from being struck by how much she reminded me of Lynn Redgrave and Jean Shrimpton – I couldn't believe how enlightened and knowledgeable she was for her age," remembered Tfank later. "How can you be that full of self-assurance when you're barely out of your teens?" Tfank wanted to know how Adele liked to look and feel while on stage. "She had this very cool beehive hair from the night before and that inspired me, too." And the designer had a very particular Hollywood icon in mind when musing on how to dress Adele. "She is more like Marilyn Monroe, who said, 'This is who I am'. She needs to show... not hide her body," was Tfank's verdict.

It would be wrong to give the impression that Adele was a complete ingénue style-wise. Even prior to the Grammys, she was aware of designer labels, aside from the long-admired Burberry. "'Something by Michael Kors – I love him – or Donna Karan," she had replied when asked what she might wear to the ceremony, prior to Anna Wintour stepping in. And she had also already made a few fashion resolutions.

Once a fan of colour in her wardrobe, she had decided that the way forward was black, and lots of it. Not a very original fashion choice you might think; but actually it was partly a musical decision. Adele had discovered Johnny Cash – 'The Man in Black' - and June Carter

Cash, and admired their pared-down monochrome look. There might be a few fancy clothes for Adele, but like Cash, she wasn't the sort of performer to distract from her music with rhinestone and fringes.

Adele was pleased with Barbara Tfank's ideas for her, pronouncing her proposed Grammy frock "really nice". "I don't ever wear dresses. Well… I wear dresses with tights and flat shoes and a cardigan. But I am going to get my boobs out and everything. It's going to be quite a big deal," she said beforehand. The dress was a very glamorous, black satin princess-line gown with three-quarter sleeves, cinched in with a belt, and teamed with a vintage diamond brooch at the bottom of its deep v-shaped neckline to show off her décolletage; opaque black tights and black Manolo Blahnik high heels with diamanté buckles. Underneath, a pair of Spanx shapewear. And to wear on top for her red carpet entrance, a camera-catching coat in an electric shade of chartreuse green.

The whole ensemble suited Adele's curvaceous figure rather well. But it didn't entirely suit Adele, who wasn't yet accustomed to this kind of dressing up and the sacrifices to comfort that it required. At the first opportunity, she undid the belt, and kicked off her shoes. It was in this relaxed state of dress that she learned she had won the Grammy for Best New Artist. After the ceremony, she told an interviewer that she liked her dress, but couldn't wait to wriggle out of her annoying Spanx and back into her jeans. "I like looking nice, but I always put comfort over fashion," she had remarked, just before the Grammys, and she was true to her word.

"Surreal" was how Adele described the whole experience afterwards, when she was safely back in her jeans. She couldn't imagine that her foray into bespoke dressing would ever be repeated. "I thought I'd be the last person that Anna Wintour would want to have anything to do with. That look will never happen again. That was a complete one-off."

But for all her protestations, Adele had learned some useful lessons from Wintour, Bowles and Tfank. "Before, I was like, 'What's the point of me going to Chanel because their sizes aren't going to fit me?' But [they] taught me to be more intelligent about dressing my figure. It's all about necklines and not trying to squash your boobs down, but showing them off!" Tfank had, she said "brought out that thing of me wanting to dress up".

It wasn't long before Adele started to take some pleasure in putting her new-found penchant for dressing up into practice. Tellingly, in her next glossy magazine interview for *Nylon* shortly afterwards, she could "rattle off the names of her favourite labels – Moschino, Donna Karan, Chanel, and Mulberry – like a seasoned pro". Adele had clearly had a bit of a fashion epiphany as far as labels were concerned. In the photographs to accompany the interview, Adele's curvy silhouette and copper hair are nicely accentuated by waist-defining clothes in shades of navy blue by Marc Jacobs, TSE and Calvin Klein. In one shot, she has characteristically kicked off her vertiginous turquoise Christian Louboutin heels to stand in her stocking feet. Killer heels notwithstanding, Adele was getting to like dressing up. Away from home, and performing in New York on her 21st birthday in May 2009, she bought herself a diamond ring from Tiffany's.

Adele's evolving attitude to clothes is summed up in an interview she gave to *Hollywood Worx* ahead of her Hollywood Bowl concert in June 2009, conducted while wearing a striped H&M baggy sweater over black American Apparel leggings, and Chanel ballerina flats. While declaring that she would "much rather dress comfortable than become a trendsetter", she once again showed that she was getting very conversant with designer labels, especially Donna Karan, Moschino, and Vivienne Westwood, which she once again cited as her favourites. Adele was also developing something of a shoe-and-bag addiction, specifically to Louis Vuitton, Gucci, Manolo Blahnik and Chanel. Although she owned up to getting "bored of things after two months", she was cultivating an eye for investment pieces. Of her seven Chanel handbags she remarked: "They'll be nice to have when I'm older. My favourite Chanel I could probably still buy in 30 years."

Despite new-found fashion wisdom, there was no danger of Adele becoming a slave to labels. "I love looking like a drag queen," she declared in the same interview. "Hair backcombed beyond belief, eyelashes galore, heavy contour. And I love my big, square, ghetto nails." "It's clear she's patrolling the border between streetwise girl and glamorous woman," said the interviewer, summing Adele's attitude up rather well. And when pressed to name those whose look inspired her, Adele came up a gutsy cast of self-assured women: Beyoncé; Sarah Jessica Parker; Sharon Stone in *Casino*, Julia Roberts in *Erin Brockovich* and Michelle Pfeiffer in *Scarface*. "The most important thing is the way that someone carries themselves. If they feel comfortable, they carry themselves differently." It was a clear signal that, though she might consent to wear clothes conferred on her by designers, she wasn't going to be anybody's clothes horse.

Barbara Tfank created another curve-enhancing dress for Adele for her landmark concert at the Hollywood Bowl in June 2009: a flocked black taffeta three-quarter-length sleeved dress with a deep neckline. With Adele's inspiration, Etta James, having pulled out due to illness, it wasn't quite the night everyone had anticipated, but Adele commanded the huge stage, helped perhaps by her glamorous dress, but not her high-heeled shoes. By the end she had taken them off to sing barefoot, a concession to comfort that would come to be a regular feature of her live shows.

Barbara Tfank continued to enjoy creating outfits for her, however. In an interview for *Vogue* in 2011, she cited Adele as one of fashion's most inspiring names to dress. "Adele is a lioness. She has poise, taste, humour and soul. Her astonishing talent never ceases to fill me with enthusiasm. I always take her lead and know I can trust her instincts - as Adele prefers black, I design for her as if she were starring in a black and white movie."

Adele's growing success, and packed schedule, coupled with her increased awareness of fashion led her to engage a stylist – Gaelle Paul – by the summer of 2009, to help her choose what to wear. "The first time I met Adele she was in this incredible Ralph Lauren poncho," said Paul. "She was like, 'Can you believe my friends said this looks like a dishcloth?' I thought, 'She's rad!'" Paul said that she had been picking out some simple dresses from Prada for Adele, and labels like Isabel Marant for her "hippy side". And then there was couture. "Anything Chanel fits her like a glove." In a few short months, Adele had been transformed from the shy girl of the early days, who would perch cross-legged on a stool in floral prints and cardigans in dingy London clubs, into a continent-conquering young woman, comfortable in couture, and in constant demand to show off clothes that other normal-shaped women might even be able to wear too.

Despite all this, Adele was at pains to make it clear that fashion, while fun, would never dominate her life. She was certainly determined not to sell out. "If they give me free stuff, I have to wear it. But I'm not into being an advertising board," she said. Neither had she become too vain of her appearance to let on about the trials and tribulations that dressing up for the occasion sometimes caused her. In January 2011, for example, *The Sun* reported Adele telling it that New Year's Eve had been a disaster because she had fallen down a hill in her Moschino outfit and heels on the stroke of midnight, and ended up "covered in dog dirt". As a consequence, instead of being out "for three days", she had been tucked up in bed by 1.30 a.m.

At the *Glamour* Awards in London in June 2009, Adele turned up to accept her award for UK Solo Artist of the Year in a black sparkly dress with gold earrings, her hair pulled back into an elegant chignon. Gone were the toppling buns of the past; but she certainly let her hair down in an interview after the ceremony. "This is how comfortable you feel," quipped the interviewer, noticing that Adele was shoeless on the red carpet. Adele quickly confessed to having fallen over on the way into the venue, in front of the paparazzi. "I just thought, 'Oh fuck it.' So I took 'em off. I've only got rainbow flats with me… and they're not really going to go with my ensemble are they?"

By the summer of 2011, performing in her stocking feet had become the norm for Adele. While she'd invariably totter on stage in high heels, the shoes would rarely last long. Kicking them off felt like a way of getting cosy with the audience while staying comfortable herself. Reviewing her gig at London's Roundhouse in July 2011, *The Observer* wrote that, "The matey chat is of [her] infamous exes, of watching Beyoncé's performance at Glastonbury on TV, and the pinch of her high heels… At the end, Adele scurries off, barefoot, before emotion can get the better of her."

Shoeless she may be prefer to be these days, but Adele still cuts a glamorous figure on stage with her sixties-inspired look. And despite the designers queuing up to dress her, she has even managed on occasion to indulge that love of vintage clothing, honed during her Camden Market days. At a gig in Seattle in August 2011, she told the audience that her elegant black dress had come from a second-hand store in California and had cost her the princely sum of $10.

Despite her voice problems, Adele looks radiant on stage in the 2011 *Live the Royal Albert Hall* DVD, with her big hair and smoky eyes, and those fabulous nails. Performing in Manchester a couple of nights before, she had showed off a "strawberry and cream" set, telling the audience that "I don't play the guitar any more because I'd rather have long nails". "I feel like a woman when I've got 'em on," she told *Q* magazine, before bursting out, "Shit! I've just broke me nail!" showing that she was just as incident prone with her talons as when that tampon had been pressed into unfortunate service.

As is seemingly inevitable for any full-fledged female celebrity these days, Adele's every outfit is now under scrutiny from the fashion-pack bloggers who are poised to comment every time she puts her toe out of the door. There have been designated hits, like this thumbs-up for her outfit for the Royal Variety Performance in December 2010: "Songbird Adele looked demure in a patterned black dress and nude Christian Louboutin Mary-Jane heels. Very pretty make-up Adele, top marks."

And there have been outfits which split opinion like the scalloped lace Barbara Tfank dress she wore to the MTV Music Video Awards in August 2011. "Not only did Adele tear down the VMAs with a heart-wrenching version of 'Someone Like You' – sans Auto-Tune, Pitbull, or harness-aided aerial somersaults – but she also brought a level-headed grace to the evening's array of looks in a demure Barbara Tfank midi-length dress. She was ravishing, hyberbole-free, and a reminder that less will always be more (provided the fit is killer)," was the verdict of *Rolling Stone*.

Elsewhere however, the view of her VMA ensemble was that understatement was, well, just... understatement. "Adele wore the exact same black shift dress you've seen her wear in every other public appearance she's ever made," declared *The Examiner*. "Granted, the crooner has an understated style, but the VMA red carpet usually calls for something a little bit spicier than something snatched from Miss Ellie rack in the *Dallas* costume-storage closet." Miaow.

Perhaps Adele's own attitude to her handbags and gladrags is best typified by remarks she made in an interview with *Rolling Stone* in April 2011. Wearing a black turtle-neck sweater she dubbed "my shield, my comfort", she said: "My life is full of drama, and I don't have time to worry about something as petty as what I look like... I don't make music for eyes. I make music for ears."

Chapter 5

Dog Days

But of course, it ended, like always. And when it did, it was like a tap turning on.

Adele, 2011

XL elected to take a relaxed attitude to the time the new album might require. "They know I won't deliver if I'm under pressure. I put the most pressure on myself anyway… I just immersed myself in this record so much that I didn't really think about the success of the first album," commented Adele. This was fortunate. For the gestation of *21* was to prove protracted, and even more fraught with emotion than that of *19*.

In the summer of 2009, after a holiday in Portugal ("It's boiling. I've got heat rash. Sunbathing's so boring!"), Adele finally got the dog she had been talking of ever since the Grammys but hadn't been home enough to consider nurturing. She reported on her blog on August 9 that she and the "doglet" – a Dachshund – were "bonding". "He is too cute; he's so friendly and loves everyone he's met so far."

The dog decided his own name by howling along while Adele was at home, singing along to a Louis Armstrong and Ella Fitzgerald track. Louie Armstrong – the quirky change of spelling was Adele's idea – he became: "But I only call him Louie Armstrong when he's naughty," she said.

By this time she moved back in with her mum, into a new flat she had bought for them in Battersea, south-west London, opposite the park and therefore handy for dog-walking. Her Notting Hill days had been short-lived. "I moved out and tried to be all cool and student-esque and I couldn't do it, and [my mum] couldn't do it either. Plus I wasn't very good at the housework."

Also a member of the new household, of course, was Louie. His stomach was soon benefitting from Adele's early attempts at baking, dog biscuits being at the top of her list. Having been away from home for so much of the previous year, Adele enjoyed the experience of being a domestic goddess. "I got loads of cookery books," she said, "and it was just me and my little dog hanging out together."

The biscuits must have been some consolation for Louie when it was time for Adele to get back to the music. She was hard at work on her new album, but could only try things out on the piano because Louie didn't like her guitar-playing. "He gets scared and I don't want to upset him." In fact, Louie would become her almost constant and loyal companion – more constant and loyal, certainly, than the men in her life.

When she had started writing her new album in earnest in early 2009, Adele was still in her "first, real relationship" with the older man, her passion for whom had caused so much emotional turmoil the previous summer, and who was at least partly responsible for her cancelled US tour. "He made me an adult. He put me on the road that I'm travelling on," was how Adele later summarised their relationship. According to what she told *Rolling* Stone in 2011, they were together for something over a year, sharing Adele's flat in London when she was in town, before it all started to fall apart. "It just stopped being fun…"

The exact duration of their relationship is shrouded in mystery however. Adele, so forthcoming on so many topics, never referred to this significant man in her life, either on her blog, or in interviews while they were together. He is conspicuous by his absence: surprising, some might think, for a man she has often called "the love of her life". Adele was toing and froing to the US more or less constantly during the period they were a couple, and one imagines this can't have been easy. In Adele's US *Vogue* interview earlier in 2009, Hamish Bowles refers to the man who had been with her in LA at the time of the Grammys in February as "her new beau, a soft-spoken London lad with the looks of Michael York in *Cabaret*"; and though not so new, we have to assume this is the same man. But back in London a few days later, Adele told Radio 1's Sara Cox that she didn't have a boyfriend. After spilling the beans on her close encounter with Justin Timberlake at the Grammys ("he's fit"); she admitted to preferring "this other boy" that she fancied. "Not a famous boy. I'd never go out with a famous boy ever." It's hard not to read these remarks now as diversionary tactics to prevent the press from getting too close to the truth. For the older man was with her at the Brits a week or so later. Adele remembered that only too well when she got up to sing 'Someone Like You' at the same awards ceremony two years later. That's why she started crying, and took half the nation down with her.

All Adele would say later was that the first song she wrote for *21* – 'Take It All' – was completed in April 2009 when she and her boyfriend were still together. Tellingly, it was about "someone not loving you". With lyrics full of hurt and desperation, of unrequited passion, it was a clear lamentation for her increasingly troubled relationship. "He did it after he heard this song," Adele would say of the break-up, with a hollow laugh when introducing 'Take It All' on tour the following year. When it came, sometime in April 2009, the split was shattering.

Studio sessions with various producers over the preceding months had yielded little that Adele was happy with; not surprising given that she was in the throes of relationship problems that were looking terminal. Then, the day after the definitive break-up, she went into the studio with songwriter and producer Paul Epworth, who had worked with the likes of Kate Nash, Primal Scream, Florence + The Machine and, most recently, Jack Peñate, with whom he had co-written and recorded Peñate's second album, *Everything Is New*.

When Jonathan Dickins had first suggested that Adele work with Epworth too, her initial reaction – thinking of his overwhelmingly indie credentials – had been, "'Well, this ain't going to work.' But I thought I'd go and get a bit drunk with him, and so we went to the pub." Luckily they hit it off, and Adele changed her mind.

Another songwriter might have looked at the state Adele was in, and sent her back under the duvet with her box of Kleenex. But Epworth could see that she was fired up in a way that might produce something rather interesting. "I never get angry, but I was ready to murder. I went in crying and stuff, and said, 'Let's write a ballad.'" And he was like, 'Absolutely not! I want to write a fierce tune.'" Epworth exhorted Adele to "be a bitch about it". "When I'm about to get angry in my heart, I can really feel my blood flowing around my body... And I kept going, 'Feel my heartbeat Paul!' And the beat of the song was my heartbeat... It just built and built."

And so 'Rolling In The Deep' was born.

"She was obviously quite fragile and very open about what had happened. But she had fire in her belly," was how Epworth later recalled the emotionally charged day-and-a-bit it took to record the track. Adele had intended it to be just a demo, but she quickly came to realise she would struggle to recapture the "heat of the moment" emotion of that first recording. So the demo became the final track; and later one of her biggest hits worldwide; and then her first US number one. Reflecting on the song's origins for her own website, Adele summed up 'Rolling In The Deep' as her reaction to "being told that my life was going to be boring and lonely and rubbish, and that I was a weak person if I didn't stay in the relationship. I was very insulted, and wrote that as a sort of 'Fuck you'."

With the recording of that fuck-you opening track, something of the steelier, more defiant character of the second album started to emerge. On tour in Canada at the beginning of May 2009, Adele told CBC Arts Online that her new record wasn't "as pathetic as the first. This one is more like, 'All right then, it's over, fuck off out my house, pack your bags, get out of my bed'." With a packed schedule, and an album to write, Adele was having to harden her centre. She couldn't expect much sympathy from those around her in any case, for she was the one and only person sad to see the back of that man. "All my friends, everyone I worked with, no one liked him, because I acted different when I was around him."

Having previously thought she "had nothing to write about", the songs started to pour out of her, just as they had done for *19*. By June, Adele was halfway through writing the album, owning up to the press that her relationships were once again providing the inspiration for her songs. "Boys," she told one interviewer when asked what she was writing about. "I've still got the same problems. In fact they're worse these days."

One consolation came in the shape of another award: Solo Artist of the Year at the *Glamour* Awards in early June, presented to her by her pal, Mark Ronson. Adele revealed around this time that she was keeping her awards, including her brace of Grammys, in the bathroom as was "traditional" in England. "I've got a big cabinet on the wall. It's funny, I was seeing this guy last summer, and he had no idea who I was. We never spoke about music… But the first time he came to my house, he went to the toilet, and when he came out he said, 'Who the fuck <u>are</u> you?'" He was so scared, she never saw him again.

June also saw the release of Jack Peñate's *Everything Is New*, co-written and produced by Paul Epworth. In an unplanned collaboration – she just happened to be around – Adele had contributed backing vocals for the song 'Every Glance'. It was clear that her own second album was going to take its time. "I'm writing the songs now, and then I'll want to rehearse them for a while," Adele said in another interview around this time. "As much as I love my first album, there are still things that I wish I had done differently. So I don't want to rush anything. You're only as good as your last record."

Actually, Adele dearly wanted the new album to be better than her last one. She had particularly taken to heart the reviews of *19* which expressed the view that her songs were not as sophisticated as her voice. "I was like, 'Right… I want to make records forever. I don't want to be a flash in the pan.' I really want to show development in my records."

With the transatlantic shuttling at an end for a while, Adele stayed put in London. She decided that the key to developing her music was to "literally lock myself into my [London] flat… and listen to all kinds of music". After two years of almost constant public appearances, Adele effectively went into hiding. "I made a huge effort to just swim in music for a while. I… sat in my house for three weeks and didn't really leave apart from to take the dog for a walk, and just listened to loads of music, catalogues of music. Loads of hip-hop, loads of country, loads of pop, loads of stuff I like already, loads of stuff I don't even like… just trying to understand what it is about that song that moves me; where it peaks, why I think it peaks, stuff like that."

There was one brief foray back to the US in September 2009, to perform at the Brooklyn Academy of Music in New York for the VH1 *Divas* event, a concert to raise money for the Save The Music Foundation charity. Adele's fellow headliners were Jordin Sparks; *American Idol* winner Kelly Clarkson; Jennifer Hudson; Miley Cyrus and Leona Lewis. Adele gave another spine-tingling rendition of 'Hometown Glory', and then later went back on stage to accompany American soul and R&B singer India Arie in her feisty song 'Video'. Despite their contrasting styles – Arie in soul chick shorts, head scarf and giant hoop earrings; Adele in black evening frock and heels – the two divas blended perfectly in a performance which oozed girl power. Adele enjoyed herself immensely, grooving to Arie's reggae beat. No wonder: 'Video' could have been written especially for her. "I'm not the average girl from your video/And I ain't built like a supermodel/But I learned to love myself unconditionally/ Because I am a queen."

And on October 7, back in her hometown, there was a further night of glory in the shape of the BMI London Awards, given annually for the year's most-performed songs on US radio and television. At the "very posh" ceremony, Adele was presented with her Award for 'Chasing Pavements', one of the three songs she had co-written for *19* with Francis 'Eg' White.

Worried about making '*19* 2.0', Adele had already decided that more such collaborations were exactly what her new album needed. "When I was doing *19*, I was a typical stubborn teenager. I was like, 'No, I can do it all on my own!'" Gradually, she was embracing the fact that she couldn't do it solo any more. A little of the creative control she guarded as fiercely as any great songwriter would have to be ceded to collaborators who could lend a fresh perspective, and help transform the "drunken diary writings" which inspired her songs into the constituent parts of a record she could be proud of.

Between November 2009 and February 2010, Adele continued to nurse her broken heart, and the rest of the songs were written. Later she reflected again on the difference between the relationship that inspired *19*, and that which had fuelled *21*. "This time, nobody did anything wrong. We just fell out of love with one another and I had to deal with the devastation of feeling like a failure because I couldn't make things work," she said. "I felt bitter, and that inspired me. But the album isn't just me bitching about an ex-boyfriend. I've also written songs in which I'm trying to be honest about my own flaws."

Chapter 6

California Blue

I think I'm a better songwriter than I thought I was.

Adele, 2010

The end of 2009 brought Adele another Grammy nomination. This time it was for Best Female Pop Vocal Performance for 'Hometown Glory'. Preoccupied with writing the new album, she chose not to attend the LA ceremony the following January, despite being up against a clutch of her heroines: Beyoncé, Katy Perry, Taylor Swift and Pink, who had so inspired her when she was a teenager. In the event it was Beyoncé who triumphed for her song 'Halo'.

After the emotional early studio session that had produced 'Rolling In The Deep', Adele had continued working with songwriter/producer Paul Epworth. "It's been an exciting experience working with someone like her and just writing. Being like, 'Here you go, here's the song'," he said. But in February, Epworth let slip that Rick Rubin was also to be involved on the album. "I've been working with Adele, just writing, not production," he told BBC6 Music at the Music Producers Guild Awards, where he won Producer of the Year. "Rick Rubin's going to be producing her next record."

This was quite a thing. Rick Rubin was a legend, but not for working with anyone like Adele. Hired by Columbia, Adele's US record company, as co-president in 2007, to help find some musical answers to their plummeting revenues, he had also variously been dubbed one of the "most infamous producers of modern music", a "hit man", a "guru" and a "medium-size bear with a long, grey beard". Oh, and also one of *Time* magazine's '100 Most Influential People in the World'.

But there were detractors. At the very awards ceremony where Epworth had revealed his collaboration with Adele, Rubin – who wasn't present despite being named International Producer of the Year – was given a slating by Matt Bellamy of Muse. On stage to accept the band's award for UK Single of the Year, he said: "We'd like to thank Rick Rubin for teaching us how not to produce."

Adele's first encounter with Rubin on *Saturday Night Live* some 18 months earlier had left her with a considerably more favourable impression of the man. She was, she said, "star struck". Then when she scooped her Grammys, Rubin sent Adele an e-mail saying, "Shall we do a record together?" Adele's reply was, "Nah, you're all right". She was concerned that the two would not be able to work together. "I didn't think we'd fit in together at all, actually."

Then Rubin came along to her show at the Hollywood Bowl in June 2009, and told her what he thought. "He said, 'You're so different live. You've got to get your live show across on your record.'" Despite his earlier offer, Adele was still shy of suggesting that they hook up. "I felt like going, 'Do you want to do it, Rick?' But I was like, 'No, I can't say that to Rick Rubin.' He'd be like, 'Do you know who I am?' But I tried to mentally plant the seed."

Eventually however, the collaboration came together when in April 2010, Adele flew out to California to record with Rubin at the Shangri-La Studios in Malibu, his favourite recording hangout. "I think it was a challenge for both of us, and I think that's why we both wanted to do it." Initially, Adele wasn't keen to record in the US, "because I'm British, and because the record is written about stuff that happened in London". But then she relented, realising that if she recorded it all at home, she would get distracted and be tempted to go out every night.

The Shangri-La Studios are something of a legend in the music business. They are housed in a modest-by-Malibu-standards mansion, built in the late fifties by a Hollywood actress named Margo Albert. It has served variously as a playground for the stars of the fifties, a film set, and – it is rumoured – as an upmarket bordello. In the seventies, music studios were installed by record producer Rob Fraboni, to the specification of Bob Dylan, who later lived in a tent in the rose garden while working there.

Over the years, the studios, which house a huge collection of guitars and vintage recording equipment, have played host to a wide variety of artists, including Van Morrison, Ringo Starr, Bonnie Raitt, Kings of Leon and Eric Clapton, who recalled it as a place where "all-night jam sessions and wild parties were the norm". The cover art for his 1976 album *No Reason To Cry* was shot inside the house. One of the few remaining analogue studios available, Shangri-La has two recording spaces: a larger one on the lower level of the house, and a smaller one in the vintage Airstream trailer parked on the lawn. There are also wonderful views of the Pacific Ocean.

Hanging out at the Shangri-La Ranch was an experience Adele was positively looking forward to after months spent lying low in London sombrely mourning her failed relationship. But the five weeks she spent in Malibu turned out not to be everything that California dreaming is cracked up to be. For a start, the fair-skinned Adele struggled with the climate. "I'm too pale for the sun. I'm allergic to it. I get heat rash," she said. "I get blisters all over me. The first day it was overcast. I got sunburnt quite badly, which lasted the entire time."

And although Adele felt right at home at Shangri-La itself, she was uncomfortable in Malibu. "It was a very surreal experience. Everyone lives behind a gate as they have so much money they don't leave... Everyone has to drive there. I thought I would walk to a cute little waterfront cafe and hang out, but you can't walk anywhere." At times, she felt unbearably homesick for London, and the familiar street ways of her hometown.

But working with the sometimes controversial Rick Rubin turned out to be a joy. "When he's speaking, you just can't help but listen," she told spin.com. "He was just so wise. I've actually never been so chilled out, being involved in music, as I was… in Malibu with him and the band." Rubin bonded with Adele by homing in on the essence of her work. "Everything I do whether it's producing, or signing an artist, always starts with the songs," he once said. "When I'm listening, I'm looking for a balance that you could see in anything. Whether it's a great painting or a building or a sunset. There's just a natural human element to a great song that feels immediately satisfying. I like the song to create a mood."

In Adele's case the essence meant that spellbinding quality which she brought to her live performances. "Her voice is a direct conduit between who she is and what we hear; there's nothing that gets in the way," was how Radio 1 DJ Zane Lowe had once aptly described it. "You can feel her life force through her voice," was Rubin's own assessment. Rubin's methods were intense, but Adele understood perfectly what he was trying to do. It chimed with the raw Etta James spirit that still burned within her. "It's all about the song, all about the music. It's so isolating in the studio, but in a really great way. We just vibed until it felt right." That involved a lot of improvising with the session band that Rubin had assembled, "insane" musicians, Adele said, so good "you could smell how great they were". "We'd listen to the songs once, and then come and jam it for about an hour, and by the end of that hour there's a take, and something great," she said in an interview recorded on location at Shangri-La. "Everyone's just so great at what they do. There's no wasted time. If you want a different sound on the guitar, it's there within 10 seconds because everyone can read each other's minds."

Crucially, this honed-down process was also kept watertight from any commercial pressures that might leak in; remarkably so, given that Rubin was co-president of Adele's US record company. "There was no 'listen up' referencing to things in the charts that were doing well and what was hot and what was not." And no samples were used in the making of the songs either. "I could sit here now, and play the whole record without electricity; it was just so organic."

The Shangri-La sessions with Rick Rubin resulted in four of the tracks that appear on *21*: 'Don't You Remember', 'He Won't Go',

'One And Only' and Adele's cover of 'Lovesong' by The Cure. The latter song happened almost by default. The most testing day in the studio came when Adele tried to record a version of 'Never Tear Us Apart' by INXS, and the Etta spirit temporarily deserted her. "It's the first song I ever learned to play, and it's one of my favourite songs," she said later of the track, which had been released the year she was born. "But when we covered it, I was devastated because I sounded so unconvincing in it. I didn't believe a word I was singing." Then, her session guitarist, Smokey Hormel, suggested doing 'Lovesong' by The Cure instead.

Adele was a long way from Finsbury Park. But at the mention of The Cure, she was transported back there. 'Lovesong' was a song she had long been familiar with, thanks to her mum and that first gig she took her infant daughter to. Hormel knew that Rubin had a demo of the song, which Rubin had originally arranged for Barbra Streisand employing shades of bossa nova, and then never used.

It was right at the end of Adele's stay in Malibu, and her voice was showing the strain of five weeks of constant jamming. But she recorded the song in one take. "It's very raw, and I'm very sad on it because I'm missing home... and the whole experience of being in Malibu with Rick Rubin was a bit overwhelming. My voice had gone, which I was a bit paranoid about. But it actually suits the song really, really well. That song set me free a little bit. I sang it for my mum." Adele's mum, however, was initially mortified at the thought of a favourite track by a beloved band getting the bossa nova treatment. "Then I played it for her. And she loved it and she cried."

Despite her sunburn, homesickness and avowed dislike of Malibu itself, the artily shot, black-and-white silent films of Adele on location at Shangri-La, later used to promote her album, are testament to a different state of mind. Here she is. Writing thoughtfully in a sun-dappled corner by the window. Dozing on the sofa, with her hair dancing lightly in the breeze. Chatting earnestly to Rick Rubin; smiling at him with her headphones on; hugging him. Smoking in the doorway and swaying to some internal beat. Jamming on the guitar. Laughing and larking around in the backyard. Lying in bed with no make-up on and a faraway look in her eyes. Pointing out of the open window across the Californian countryside. Driving along the Pacific Highway, glamorous in over-sized shades like a movie star of old. Cuddling up close to the camera and flirting with it, making smiling eyes through long, dark, luxuriant lashes. She looks beautiful, relaxed and very her. And as if something has been fulfilled musically.

In May 2010, Adele came to the end of her time at Shangri-La and flew home to London. "I had a great time in Malibu," she wrote later on her blog. "It was all a bit overwhelming getting to work with such amazing people who just ooze greatness. It was like living with my fantasy family for a month."

Because of his super-producer status within the music industry, Adele's work with Rick Rubin has tended to grab the headlines. With him, she had recorded four of the 11 tracks which would appear on *21*. But back in London the work continued, with hometown collaborators who were to play just as crucial a role in the eventual runaway success of the album. And despite all the great music that had resulted from her time in Malibu, Adele was keen to stay put and work in London for a while. "I didn't want to be travelling loads, back and forth, to write. I just wanted to be at home around my comforts and around my friends."

The crossovers between Adele's co-writers and producers on *21* are fascinating, with stimulating combinations emerging in the process. After their successful collaboration on the first album track, 'Rolling In The Deep', Adele wrote two more songs with Paul Epworth: 'He Won't Go' and 'I'll Be Waiting'. Epworth also produced 'I'll Be Waiting', while, as already noted, Rubin handled 'He Won't Go'. Despite her initial reservations about working with Epworth, "It ended up a match made in heaven," she said. "He's one of the most amazing writers and producers I've ever worked with; he's got so many ideas and he brought a lot out of me."

Adele's work on *21* also reunited her with Jim Abbiss, whom she had worked with on eight of the 12 tracks on *19*. For *21*, Abbiss produced 'Take It All', co-written with Francis 'Eg' White – another of Adele's producers from *19* – and also 'Turning Tables', co-written by Adele with US songwriter and producer Ryan Tedder. Adele's collaboration with Tedder came about after an encounter in a lift at the Grammy Awards in LA in 2009. "We were both staying in the same hotel, and I got in the elevator with about 100 heart balloons. And then Ryan got in as well, and all he could hear was my cackle, which I think has become a bit infamous! And he was searching through all the balloons to find me, and we were like, 'Amazing! We've definitely got to work together now'."

Frontman of rock band OneRepublic, and recipient of awards for his work on such Adele-revered tracks as Beyoncé's 'Halo' and 'Bleeding Love' by Leona Lewis, Tedder was in some ways an obvious candidate to collaborate with Adele. To start with, however, she wasn't even sure she liked him. After that initial meeting at the Grammys, they got together over a meal in New York City. "I was, like, 'Who the fuck does he think he is?'" she recalled. But by the end of the meal, they had, appropriately enough, "turned the table upside down".

The collaboration came off because rather than impose his own style, Tedder was keen just to let Adele be Adele. As he explained: "*19...* was so absolutely mind-blowing to me, so simple and beautiful, that I don't want myself, as a fan, to interfere with her sound." Tedder told Adele that he didn't want to put her "through the Ryan Tedder machine where you end up with a song that sounds as much like Ryan Tedder as it does Adele". 'Rumour Has It' was written and produced with Tedder in the US, while 'Turning Tables' was written in London and then produced by Jim Abbiss.

'Set Fire To The Rain', meanwhile, was the result of Adele's collaboration with Fraser T Smith. Smith first came to prominence as Craig David's guitarist, and had since gone on to pen hits for the likes of James Morrison and Tinchy Stryder. He and Adele worked together at the suggestion of her manager, Jonathan Dickins, who reported that Smith and Adele "just clicked. He is ambitious, has a great work ethic, a great pop sensibility, and... is an absolute perfectionist. Most of all he's a lovely guy, and very modest." Smith later described the experience of listening to Adele laying down her extraordinary, emotive vocal for 'Set Fire To The Rain' as "amazing". But it wasn't a typical recording session. "Louie, her really sweet little dog, was barking through the whole take," he said, "and I was sort of pacifying the dog, picking him up, and he was weeing a bit everywhere."

The final songwriter/producer with whom Adele worked on the album was Dan Wilson. It was Rick Rubin's idea to put her together with the LA-based Wilson, who could boast a long and varied career in music, both writing and performing his own work - notably on his 2007 album, *Free Life,* which he also produced with the help of Rubin – and writing for the likes of The Dixie Chicks, KT Tunstall and Carole King. Adele was, Wilson said, "already totally on my radar" from her début album. Together they wrote 'One And Only', 'Don't You Remember' and 'Someone Like You' for *21*, the former also with input from US songwriter Greg Wells. "Adele truly is the most talented person I've ever written with," said Wells. "To have her sing her ideas sounding the way she sounds, it's kind of spoiled me forever." Wilson was equally impressed. "She is a very visionary artist," he said. "She knows exactly what she wants. She's doesn't mess around. She's really funny and a good hang, but she knows exactly what she wants to do."

'Someone Like You' would be the last track on the album, but it was actually Adele's first collaboration with Wilson. In summing up what it was like to work with Adele in an interview after *21* was completed, Wilson quoted a remark of Rick Rubin's. "He said something very true about her. She's very, very spontaneous with writing lyrics." And so it was with 'Someone Like You'. Adele had discovered via a text from a friend late one night that her ex boyfriend – *the* ex boyfriend, whom she had been so intensely thinking, writing and singing about - had become engaged to another woman. Utterly crushed, she instinctively sought some kind of musical comfort. She was sitting on the end of her bed, waiting for her bath to run, and reached for her acoustic guitar. Within minutes, she had composed most of the lyrics to 'Someone Like You'. Shortly afterwards, she went to Dan Wilson and asked him to help finish the song she had written so rapidly and instinctively. It was eventually recorded and produced with Wilson in LA.

Months later, with Adele's album riding high in the charts around the world, Wilson reflected on the songs they had composed together. "I've listened to *21* a lot. And I've noticed that some of the great songs on the album are very metaphorical, like 'Set Fire To The Rain' and 'Turning Tables'. The things that she and I wrote are just dead simple... They are so emotionally direct... I always hope for someone who can speak so plainly and honestly but do it in an artful way."

The composition of 'Someone Like You' was perhaps more painful than that of any other song. Adele was, she admitted, "pretty miserable and pretty lonely" when she wrote it. It was the antithesis to the ballsy, defiant 'Rolling In The Deep', and the two tracks would eventually bookend her album to signify the emotional, personal journey that the devastating break-up had sent her on. Whereas 'Rolling In The Deep' had been Adele's 'Fuck you' – a declaration that she was going to be fine without him – 'Someone Like You' was sung out of her despair.

But the track also represented a kind of catharsis for her. After she had written it, she had an overwhelming sense of shift, despite her continuing anguish about their separation. Of acceptance. "I was exhausted from being such a bitch... emotionally drained from the way I was portraying him. Because even though I'm very bitter...he's still the most important person that's ever been in my life... I had to write ['Someone Like You'] to feel OK with myself, and OK with the two years I spent with him. And when I did it, I felt so freed."

"Hello. Thinking maybe its time to slowly bring myself out of hiding." After almost 10 months of silence on her blog, Adele re-surfaced with this understated post on October 7, 2010. "I've been from Malibu to Kensal Rise over the past year and a bit... writing and singing till my heart felt like it was going to pop out my chest and start beating me up!" she said. In her spare time, she had, she reported, been discovering Wanda Jackson, playing with her dog, learning to cook, and rekindling what she called an "on-and-off relationship with gin and tonic". And there had also been a doomed attempt to learn to drive. "I didn't keep up my lessons. I was recovering from a severe break-up so I was drinking a lot [and] I imagine I was over the limit for most of them," she later confessed.

The album, however, was finished. By the autumn of 2010, plans for its release were already gaining momentum, with the full marketing might of her record company and management teams deployed to build on the achievements of *19*. The new album, to be named *21,* was a much fuller work, involving a much larger cast of collaborators and musicians. But Adele remained deeply and personally connected to it. The album was about a man: a man who used to be hers. One for whom she was later to confess, she would have given up everything, if they could only have stayed together. "Well, I would still be singing in the shower, of course, but yeah - my career, my friendships, my hobbies. I would have given up trying to be the best... I don't think I'll ever forgive myself for not making my relationship with my ex on *21* work... He's the love of my life."

If *19* had been a bittersweet teenage break-up record about the transience of first love, *21* was about grown-up pain, and an adult soul laid bare. And Adele would have to keep baring that soul. Not just on the end of the bed or into a recording studio mike, but henceforth for the world.

21: About A Woman

I was really angry. Then I was bitter. Then I was really lonely, and then I was devastated. It was in that order – the record.

Adele on *21*

21 is a big album, confident and consistent; and that is just as Adele wanted it to be. It was her ambition that it would have a greater scope than the contained, mainly acoustic *19*, but she quickly recognised that to achieve this, she would have to acknowledge her own limitations. "I do love all the acoustic stuff on my first album. But as a writer, I'm quite limited in terms of writing production stuff, arrangements and layers." She desperately wanted to prove herself a career artist, who would show growth and development with each record: *19* part two would not do.

There had been some co-writing on *19*, of course, notably with Eg White, but essentially Adele had written the songs alone and then worked up the music to differing degrees with her three producers. The story of *21* is one of collaboration at a much earlier stage. "My first record is about 80% me on my own, this one is about 60%," she said. Another artist might have found it difficult to relinquish control in this way, but the single-minded Adele was astute enough to realise that working with others would help her to look at her own work in a more objective light. "I'm quite throwaway with my own material, and I find I'm more forgiving of myself if I'm working with other people."

This did not mean that she would be content to be less of a presence on *21*. If anything, she wanted to put more of herself into it than ever before. Wary of making an emotionally one-dimensional album that would be dubbed just another "break-up" record, she was keen for it to reflect all aspects of her personality. "People always think I'm a serious person, especially off the back of *19* because it's quite a moody record.

But I'm not…When I'm not singing, I like to try and be sarcastic and cheeky and funny, and I wanted that to come across in a few new songs." The new album would, she hoped, also reflect the extent to which she had grown in confidence. "I feel a lot bolder now in terms of what the songs are about so I wanted a bit of oomph behind them." Like her first album, *21* would also chart the aftermath of a ruptured relationship, but in all its complex moods and stages. It would be less about the man who had broken her heart, than about the woman determined to survive him.

Musically, Adele had matured too. She had soaked up a plethora of new inspirations since the making of *19* and was keen to bring some of her new passions to bear on the record. But it was an Adele album she wanted, not a hotchpotch of disparate influences. She told BBC6 Music: "I'm more interested in having a body of work rather than a mishmash of sounds. I think my first album was a bit of pop, a bit of R&B, a bit of jazz, a bit of wannabe rock and a bit of indie folk… I bought all these amazing iconic albums and I'm trying to work out why they have a sound… I want an Adele sound."

In her quest for career development and that sound, Adele spent weeks at home just "swimming in music", listening both to newly acquired classic albums and to artists she had "loved forever": Mary J Blige, Kanye West, Elbow, Mos Def, Alanis Morissette, Tom Waits and Sinéad O'Connor. And in the wake of her US tour, she had dozens of new sounds to add to the mix too. Thanks to her tour bus driver, whom she refers to as B, Adele had discovered a wealth of country music artists on the long cross-country journeys between shows. Latching on to her enthusiasm, B played her record upon record; started making her compilations, including selections of early Dolly Parton, Johnny Cash and The Carter Family. Adele – who prior to this awakening had never listened to country music – was soon thrilling to the sounds of such miscellaneous artists as Loretta Lynn, Alison Krauss, Rascal Flatts, Sugarland, Neko Case, T Bone Burnett, Lady Antebellum and The SteelDrivers.

After Adele told *Rolling Stone* of her newly found love of country, the magazine excitedly reported that her forthcoming album would fall into the genre, under the headline "Adele Goes Country on Fall Disc". Adele later scotched the rumours in an interview to accompany her appearance on Radio 1's *Live Lounge* in January 2011. "I haven't made a country record... It's more about the delivery, and the manipulation of words, feelings and emotions that I like to think has rubbed off on me. But not the actual method of writing a country song. My accent doesn't suit a country song... I haven't got that twang!"

But it was also the storytelling common to many country songs which had inspired Adele. "Contemporary records can take three minutes to get to the point, and sometimes you don't know what the song is about even when it's finished. Whereas in the first 20 seconds of a country song you know exactly what's going on. I found it easy to imagine myself in those situations and kind of pick an old memory of mine and think about it as I listened. I like the feel, it's quite euphoric and triumphant-sounding but also really dangerous and bitter. It's more emotional than pop music, as emotional as the soul singers I enjoyed from when I was little."

"She'd definitely been exposed to things that opened her eyes musically," said Paul Epworth of his time working with Adele on *21*. "So much of the music from the United States over the last century was formed from various trials and tribulations, and I think that's reflected on Adele's record – that she identified with these artists singing about their lives."

But if there was one artist who stood out as an influence on *21*, it was the "wild, fierce" rockabilly pioneer Wanda Jackson, who had toured with Elvis Presley in the fifties (and briefly dated him), before moving into country and gospel later in her career. "I got really into how gritty and dirty she was; her voice is just insane." Adele loved to cite the fact that Jackson routinely introduced herself as "the angel with the dirty mouth". At the age of 73, the evergreen Jackson would later support Adele for part of her North American tour during the summer of 2011, performing some of her old hits, along with tracks from her new album, *The Party Ain't Over*, produced by Jack White, and released on the same day as *21*. A BBC review dubbed it "a sumptuous, brassy stew of country and blues".

Adele's *21* emerged over a period of roughly 18 months between April 2009 and October 2010, corresponding with another time of turmoil in her personal life. Her break-up with the most significant man she had been with to date occurred shortly after she had started work on the album, and provided much of the material for it, shaped by the musical influences she had been busy absorbing. The heady cocktail of emotions she set about reflecting on the new record was considerably more complex than that which had fuelled *19*.

Her mutable state of mind in the wake of her break-up is mirrored in the sequence of songs on the album which progressively work out her anger and bitterness; her guilt; her loneliness and desolation; and finally her readiness to move on. The process could not have been more intense, or personal. "The experience of writing this record was quite exhausting, because I would go from being a bitch to being completely on my knees. It was like the stages of my recovery."

The 10 original songs that appear on *21* were written in both London and Los Angeles, along with around five tracks which didn't make the final album. Although the greater degree of collaboration on *21* meant that she ended up travelling to the US more than she had done for *19*, Adele was relieved to be able to base herself mainly in London, particularly after a solid year of touring. "I finally was at home and had to live a bit again and decide... Well, I didn't need to decide what I was going to write about; I knew what I was going to write about."

Just as 'Chasing Pavements' had done, Adele's songs on *21* often began as what she called 'drunken diary ramblings'. But this time they were turned into dramatic, fully fledged pieces of music with the help of her six co-writers, and six producers. This cross-pollination undoubtedly contributed to making the new record a more complex whole than the more discrete creative processes which characterised the making of *19*. Adele credited all her producers for giving her the confidence to tackle her fluctuating emotions head-on. She paid tribute to Rick Rubin, in particular, for helping her relax into the process and let it take its organic course. "I'm a control freak and I don't like spontaneity," she said. "But he made me go with my instincts and loosen up as I was singing."

At the outset, however, Adele had reservations about the other producers she was being paired with. She was concerned that Paul Epworth was too "indie"; that Ryan Tedder's distinctive sound would overshadow hers; and that Rubin – a pioneer of rap and hip-hop – would be daunting to work with, and might be more absent than present. In the end however, the contra-indicative nature of the collaborations paid off handsomely, undoubtedly contributing to an album that is varied and often surprising. In their different ways, all of her producers rose to the challenge of helping Adele establish a more confident and complete sound, and one that would do justice to her considerable talents.

Although some have found certain tracks over-produced, the spontaneity of Adele's vocal response to the various stages on her emotional journey infuses the whole album. It is remarkable that even on this bigger, much more collaboratively produced album, which involved a cast list three times longer than that for *19*, a quarter of the final tracks – "Rolling In The Deep', 'Someone Like You' and 'Lovesong' – were originally recorded as demos, which everyone later decided could not be improved upon. The first two of those demos, the songs with which the album opens and closes, would become its biggest successes, and, in their very different ways, Adele's signature tunes.

On its release, the album's title provoked some jokey comment in the media. For the second album running, it was quipped, Adele had been unable to come up with anything more original than her age when she was writing it. She had in fact tried to resist the idea of calling it *21* but the idea wouldn't go away. "It was… an obvious title, but I think being obvious sometimes is right, rather than trying to be clever," she said. "Twenty-one is a really important age everywhere, and I really do feel like I've changed since turning 21 and everything that's happened. It's all quite fitting."

A certain age she may have been when she wrote it, but the huge success of *21* stems from the fact that it appeals to listeners of all ages, from pre-teens to senior citizens. As *The Guardian* put it: "People can crow at the lack of innovative sonic ideas on display, but they are not what find you an audience, from *NME*-reading teens to aunties humming along to Radio 2."

And Adele liked her album too. "I do love it. I just love the vibe of it… And I think some of the songs on here are the most articulate I've ever written."

Rolling In The Deep

'Rolling In The Deep', described by Adele as a "dark, bluesy, gospel disco tune" hits the listener hard from its first powerful beat, setting a tone of high drama for what is to follow, and immediately signalling a big shift from the pared-back acoustic sound characteristic of *19*.

The story of the song's swift and fiery genesis explains a lot. It was written and recorded with Paul Epworth, the morning after Adele had broken up with her "soul mate". Adele arrived at her scheduled recording session in a raw state of emotional upset. Instead of trying to calm her down, Epworth exhorted her to rage about it, and Adele's racing heartbeat dictated the pace for the pounding opening to the song. "I'm such a fucking drama queen. I was so angry!" she said. Blood up, she sang the first verse of the song *a cappella* while Epworth improvised the tune on his guitar. The rest followed quickly, and a demo was laid down in less than two days.

"I guess it's my equivalent of saying things in the heat of the moment, and word-vomiting," said Adele later of the track that would become the album's first single release. "It takes a lot of shit to get me a bit upset and crazy, so when I get angry in my heart, I can really feel my blood flowing around my body." Spurred on by Epworth, she had wanted to write a song that people would listen to "and be like, 'Shit, it sounds like she is going to kill him.'"

Aside from the anger that pulsates through 'Rolling In The Deep', Adele also wanted the song to reflect her cheekier side. "I'm really sarcastic, really cheeky, I'm always trying to crack a joke and make people laugh. I think 'Rolling In The Deep'…[is] more relevant to that." It is also the song on which the Wanda Jackson influence is most evident, in particular a lesser-known 1961 track beloved of Adele called 'Funnel Of Love'. "It sounds really Phil Spectory," she said, "and it rubbed off on 'Rolling In The Deep' when I started writing it."

The disco beat of 'Rolling In The Deep' was also born out of Adele's desire to have at least one or two tracks on the album which would get her concert audiences moving. "When I go and see a live show, if it's all ballads, towards the end I get really itchy legs," she said. "I thought I should throw in a couple of upbeat ones so they can kind of work their legs a little bit!"

Driven by drum and bass, and with great backing vocals, 'Rolling In The Deep' evokes high emotion in the listener, building a sense of angry foreboding. "She hooted, she hollered; she came mob-handed with a host of avenging backing doppelgangers," as *The Guardian*'s reviewer described it. But thanks to its pulsating beat, 'Rolling in Deep' is also a catchy pop song which gets the feet moving, just as Adele intended it to.

Released as a single in the UK just ahead of *21* in January 2011, 'Rolling In The Deep' was received very positively, setting the stage for the bigger sound of Adele's second album. "The single is an epic, foot-stomper of a pop anthem with thumping piano and a vocal you would expect from a veteran of 20 years on the road," said *The Sun*.

"Adele's noticeable leap in vocal confidence highlights the track," agreed *Billboard*. The verdict from *Rolling Stone* emphasised the US influences that had gone into making the record: "This breakup-mourning track builds to a stomping, hand-clapping climax that affirms the English knack for rejiggering the sound of American roots music."

Originally, Adele had thought of using 'Rolling In The Deep' as the title of the album itself, but then decided that it was "a bit of a mouthful and the Europeans would be totally baffled by it". The phrase derives from the hip-hop slang expression to "roll deep", or keep close to a person or a group, so there is always someone at your back to help you fight if you get into trouble. It reflected the doomed nature of Adele's relationship. "That's how I felt, you know, I thought that's what I was always going to have," she said. "And... it ended up not being the case."

Despite her initial doubts about what a producer with the indie pedigree of Paul Epworth could bring to her record, 'Rolling In The Deep' turned out to be "exactly the kind of thing he had in mind to do with me". Adele later paid tribute to Epworth, calling their collaboration on the album "a match made in heaven". On 'Rolling In The Deep' he had, she said, "really brought my voice out of me... There's notes I hit in that song that I never even knew I could hit." And the track indeed showcases a voice of considerable range, propelled by a confident and mature singer who is unafraid to challenge it.

Born out of a session from which a wounded and wound-up Adele expected very little, 'Rolling In The Deep' eventually went on the album in its demo form, later takes having failed to re-capture the raw emotion of that charged day in the studio. It is testament to the combined skills and focus of both Adele and Epworth that it produced the actual recording that would become such a big hit.

'Rolling In The Deep' also went on to be the most covered song on the album with artists as diverse as Patti Smith, Lil Wayne, Nicole Scherzinger, Linkin Park and the cast of *Glee* venturing their own versions. And it was a landmark song for Adele too. Rick Krim of VH1, for which Adele recorded an *Unplugged* session shortly before *21* was released in the US, was among those who felt that Adele had acquired "a little more swagger" on the new album. "A lot has happened to her since her first record, so you expect to hear some growth. The first single, it's just instantaneous – it doesn't sound like anything on her début."

Rumour Has It

"It's about this boy I met in the summer. I don't trust people very easily. Nothing really happened – we went out on a few dates. And he tried to sell his story to the fucking *Sun* newspaper!" So Adele said in a radio interview in Canada in May 2009, talking about the origins of 'Rumour Has It'. She never mentioned the boy again, but the song certainly reflects the fact that Adele's growing celebrity had brought the unwelcome attention of the tabloids. The gossip surrounding her was already such that when she returned home after long periods on tour in the US and tried to catch up with her London friends, she found that even they had started to believe the rumours. "My friends would be like, 'I heard this thing in blah, blah... I hope you're not seeing him because I hear he fucked her... and I heard you're with him.' My own friends were gossiping about me. Because it's called 'Rumour Has It', some people might think that it's about blogs and mags and papers, but it's not. It's about my own friends believing stuff that they hear."

'Rumour Has It' was written in the US with American songwriter and producer Ryan Tedder, whom Adele had first met in a lift after the Grammys in February 2009. The collaboration wasn't as random as that encounter makes it sound however: Tedder's songwriting credits included huge hits for the likes of Beyoncé, Kelly Clarkson, The Pussycat Dolls and Leona Lewis.

Admirer of his work though she was, referring to him as a "hit factory", Adele was unfazed by Tedder's reputation. From the beginning of their collaboration, she wanted them to arrive at a sound that would be distinctive to her record. "You can really tell when you hear a Ryan Tedder song. Which I liked, but I wanted something that would surprise everyone. So we came up with this sort of bluesy, pop, stomping song." It also had what she dubbed "dirty guitar".

Jazzy in vibe and powered by clapping and finger-snaps, as well as a vocal with attitude, 'Rumour Has It' features one of the album's more complex arrangements. It's a track of contrasts, too, with a dramatic bridge section that clears away everything bar some strings and sweeping piano to accompany Adele's haunting vocal, before the drums cascade back again in the final chorus. Dubbed "Motown on steroids" by one reviewer, it was also referred to as "a swamp song so perfectly shadowy David Lynch might be fond of it".

Tedder later paid tribute to the whole album and what it represented for Adele. "As much as I love *19* - and I do - this is a giant leap forward for her. With a couple of exceptions, *19* was very subdued; *21* isn't."

In contrast to the raw emotions that characterise most of the other tracks on the album, 'Rumour Has It' is a song that Adele says is, "not to be taken seriously... I was fucking hung over as well, the last thing I wanted to do was try and be emotional... It's basically me just taking the piss."

Turning Tables
Though eventually produced in London by Jim Abbiss, with whom Adele had worked so extensively on *19*, 'Turning Tables' was also co-written

with Ryan Tedder. Like 'Rolling In The Deep', the song was born out of the heat of a fight Adele had with her ex-boyfriend. In one version of the story, Adele had arrived in the studio for a scheduled session with Tedder, upset and seething after an argument with her former lover. "I didn't know Ryan at this point, and I turned up going; 'Who the fuck does he think he is, always fucking turning the tables on me?' And then he took that "turning tables" and came up with the phrase, which I loved."

In another variant on the tale, Adele said that the dispute with her ex took place outside a Chinese restaurant in New York and triggered the downfall of their relationship. They had started arguing in the Dim Sum restaurant around one of those tables that turns so that everyone can get a bit of each dish. It proved an apt metaphor: "We stormed out into the street and kept turning everything round on each other."

'Turning Tables' brings the tempo down from the driving beats of the first two tracks on the album, and creates a softer, more melancholy mood. Though more orchestral, it takes the listener back to the kind of piano and string accompaniments familiar from *19*, and has an openness in the production, typical of other Abbiss-produced tracks, which allows the full range and tone of Adele's voice to power through. Initially pared back to a minimal ballad, it swells to a cinematic, string-laden climax, while Adele's voice periodically cracks with the emotion of it all. The lingering, slowly fading strings at the end emphasise the hurt and bitterness set to continue after the song is done.

Adele's maturity of voice on the track marked her out as a singer who no longer needed comparing with anyone. "'Turning Tables' sets Adele in a class of her own, now that the critics no longer draw lazy comparisons to her early British contemporaries," as one reviewer put it. "This is a ballad that will try its hardest to raise hairs all over your body," said another.

Adele gave a memorable performance of 'Turning Tables' on *The Late Show With David Letterman* in the US and another, later, on *The Jonathan Ross Show* in September 2011, shortly before she was forced to cancel all her tour dates due to her vocal-cord problems. The strain in her voice is audible in the latter performance, but ultimately it suits the raw emotion of the song, and her rendition is chillingly good.

Don't You Remember

'Don't You Remember' is the first Rick Rubin-produced track on *21* and is one of three songs on the album co-written by US musician and songwriter Dan Wilson. It introduces a more self-reflexive tone after the fraught and heated moods of the tracks that precede it. Its lyrics suggest someone starting to calm a little and think about their own part in a difficult break-up, while looking back wistfully on the good things about their relationship, and pleading with an ex not to forget them.

The song came about when Adele, some way into her work on the album, started reflecting on some of the songs she had already written, and was struck by the negative light in which she had cast her former love. "I suddenly got really ashamed…with the manner in which I was portraying someone who was really important to me… and I felt really bad and childish that I'd made him out to be a complete twat… I started reminiscing about how at the beginning, my skin would tingle any time he ever touched me, and I'd wait by my phone going crazy because he didn't text me back within 10 seconds."

Of all the songs on the album, this ballad is one of those most obviously influenced by Adele's newly found love of country music. Acknowledging the track's "country tinge", Adele has also cited Lady Antebellum's 'Need You Now' for giving her the courage to try and do something similar musically. "When I was in the studio in Malibu, this was the last song I wrote while I was recording, and 'Need You Now' was everywhere. It's just one of those songs. The amount of times I've made a drunk fucking phone call! I've never heard two voices work so brilliantly either. It was incredible. I saw them live in Minneapolis…. and it was one of the best shows I've ever seen… But the feeling the song gave me, I was trying to channel it in my own song".

Describing the track as "very American" because "it has a key change at the end", Adele has also dubbed the song an "ode to a new discovery for me". It opens with some simple guitar arpeggios through the chord sequence and then develops into a very full sound towards its soaring climax, with the bass and drums holding down a solid backline, and the lead guitar wandering freely through the chorus, while the strings subtly colour in the remaining space.

Reviewing *21*, *The Observer* referred to 'Don't You Remember' scathingly as a "ghastly, mid-paced ballad". Elsewhere however, the verdict was that its heart-string-pulling country flavour made it one of the album's most memorable and affecting tracks: "With its mellow verses and heartfelt chorus, any listener that has been through heartbreak can relate with Adele. Ironically, this is one we definitely will remember," was MTV's verdict. One reviewer even felt that it was this song, above any other, which had finally seen off the competition: "Adele makes it seem like Duffy, Joss Stone and Amy Winehouse never happened."

Set Fire To The Rain

'Set Fire To The Rain' is the only track on the album written with British songwriter Fraser T Smith, who also produced it. He and Adele worked together at the suggestion of Adele's manager, Jonathan Dickins, who recognised among Smith's qualities "a great pop sensibility". An arresting power ballad, 'Set Fire To The Rain' is perhaps the most purely pop song on the album, and was the third and last single to be released from it after 'Rolling In The Deep' and 'Someone Like You'. The single reached number one in Poland, Belgium and the Netherlands; and number 11 in the UK following its release there in July 2011.

Signalled by the oxymoron in its title, the song was, said Adele, an attempt to convey the "contradictions that are in relationships… One person says this, the other person says that," and the way that we can have conflicting feelings about the people that we love. "I was… heartbroken when I met who the song's about, and he brought me back to life and put me back together, and he was a dickhead as well."

From its striking first line a big symphonic production characterises the song. It opens to a controlled tempo on the piano, accompanied by drums and bass, with some ethereal synth voices floating behind, underpinned by strings which flood its sweeping chorus. One reviewer remarked that the song's production recalled "elements of Phil Spector in his heyday".

The sheer power of the song split opinion on its release. Some reviewers felt that 'Set Fire To The Rain' was an overwrought production; "the only real misfire on the album". MTV was more generous, countering such criticisms by saying that although "some may say it's slightly over produced... we are still loving Adele's faultless voice, littered with sentiment." *The Guardian* referred to it, somewhat equivocally, as, "Truly a song for all shades of misery."

Adele has given other, more miscellaneous accounts of the derivation of her contrarily named song. Prior to a stirring performance on *The Graham Norton Show*, she told her fellow guests on the couch that, "It doesn't really make sense but don't worry." On another occasion, while chatting to her audience before a live performance of the song, Adele said that it was written in response to a friend telling her that 'Chasing Pavements' wasn't enough of a gay anthem. But perhaps the most random account of the song's title came during a gig in Leeds. Confirmed smoker Adele told the crowd that she had come up with the idea on a rainy day. When her lighter stopped working in the wet...

He Won't Go

After the swelling, highly strung production of 'Set Fire To The Rain', 'He Won't Go' sets an entirely different tone. Written with Paul Epworth and produced in Malibu by Rick Rubin, the inspiration for the song was not Adele's ex but two of her friends. "I was home after touring for my first record, and I'd settled into my new flat... but [I] had no normal friends in my area. It was all work friends, or people I'd met through work, and then I met these two through our mutual love of dogs." Adele soon discovered that one of her new friends was a heroin addict about to enter rehab. "Their bond with each other... overcame everything that was going on... and that really touched and moved me," she said. "He's been clean for over a year now, and it's quite exciting seeing a new life happen when you're 30-odd."

The song is also about sticking with someone, despite being told that you would be better off without them. Coincidentally – or perhaps not - this was exactly how it was for a time with Adele and her ex-boyfriend, of whom neither her friends nor her family approved.

Leanly produced by Rick Rubin, the track begins with a languid percussion line to which some sweet chords on the piano are added, before a funky bass-line kicks in. The syncopated rhythms of the chorus, and the unexpected introduction of a harp, are particularly seductive. There are strong echoes of contemporary hip-hop and R&B, which prompted comparisons for 'He Won't Go' with the work of Mary J Blige and Lauryn Hill, both singers admired by Adele.

"Adele has real chemistry with Epworth," said *Rolling Stone*, urging readers to "check his old-school/new-school magic act" on the track.

Take It All

'Take It All' reunited Adele with two of her producers from *19*: Eg White who co-wrote the song, and Jim Abbiss who produced it. The song was the first on the album to be written, and the only track to emerge from the difficult and turbulent period when Adele was in the throes of breaking up with her ex. 'Take It All' was composed in the spring of 2009 when they were still together but, she said, "It's about my devotion to someone, and them not caring, and taking the piss out of me, and exploiting me, in a way." She poured all her hurt and frustration into this wrenching lament for her increasingly troubled relationship.

Given its painful content, the track emerged remarkably quickly during a two-day session with White. Adele was feeling her way back into writing and recording after having spent so long on tour. She and White whiled away most of the first day catching up and gossiping, having not seen each other for months. It was only towards the end of the second day that work on the track began in earnest. "He played a chord, and then I just started singing it... and literally as I sang it, the lyrics sort of happened... I was really surprised about the contents. I only find out what I'm thinking and feeling in my songs. And I didn't realise I was feeling like this."

In keeping with the simplicity of its composition, the gospel-flavoured track gives Adele's soaring and passionate vocal only a simple piano accompaniment and brief snaps of backing vocals in the chorus. The result is "a gritty, raw outpouring" and one of the most affecting songs on the album. After she had written it, Adele waited a few days before playing it to her boyfriend. "He left me a couple of weeks after."

I'll Be Waiting

"It's almost like I imagined walking down the street with it on my iPod and going, 'Yeah! The soundtrack to my life!'" Co-written and produced with Paul Epworth, 'I'll Be Waiting' introduces a much more upbeat note to the album, signalling perhaps the beginning of Adele's defiant recovery from what her ex had put her through. "Every time we added something new to it, or wrote a new part, we got really excited because we were happy," she said later of working on the song with Epworth. One reviewer, picking up on the mood, described the track as "a powerful, forward looking catharsis in a sea of songs detailing heartbreak and the wreckage of relationships gone sour".

Adele's voice is a commanding presence on the track, which also features some great brass sounds. The bridge gives the listener pause for thought to really take in the lyrics, before everything drops back into the chorus with a big flourish. The whole is deeply groovy, making it another of those tracks designed to get Adele's live audiences moving their feet between ballads.

The soulful soaring of 'I'll Be Waiting' inspired reviewers to a whole host of comparisons, referring variously to its "Aretha Franklin vibe"; its "Rolling Stones-esque bar-room gospel"; and its shades of Eric Clapton, The Beatles and Dusty Springfield – as well as Adele's recent crush, Lady Antebellum.

"'I'll Be Waiting' will," said another critic, "tempt you to call your last love and leave the track playing on the voicemail, a glass of sweet-tea vodka in hand."

One And Only

Continuing the more optimistic mood, 'One And Only' found Adele thinking about a different man. "It's another happy song... about someone that I've known for years. We've always liked each other, and never been together, even though I'm pretty convinced I'm probably going to marry this guy in the end." The middle eight was written the day after Adele had spent the evening watching *Never Been Kissed* with Drew Barrymore, who describes in the film how the whole world goes blurry when she is being kissed. "It's cheesy, but whenever I hear the bridge, it is sort of like that… I just imagine being kissed, and the whole world slowing down and it being a bit like a fairy tale." The resulting song is an uncomplicated soul number; no strings or brass, just a tight song played by her Malibu band, and produced by Rick Rubin.

'One And Only' was co-written with Dan Wilson and Greg Wells. Wells described his three-day writing session with Adele in LA as unlike any other he had experienced, and he was staggered when the song seemed to emerge from Adele almost fully formed. "I heard a piano progression of four chords, and a slow 6/8 feel. I kept playing it for about 10 minutes. Adele was pacing the room with a note pad and pen… then [she] finally said, 'I'm not sure if this is good, but what do you think of this?' And then in full voice she sang the finished chorus of 'One And Only' and I almost fell over." The song needed only minimal tweaks from Dan Wilson and Adele the following week.

Later, Adele's feelings towards the potential 'one and only' she wrote it about changed completely. In New York in May 2011 she introduced the track by saying: "It's about trying to buck up the courage to tell someone who you've loved for ages that you want to be with them." But at the Royal Albert Hall in September, however, she told the audience that "this guy was a fucking prick to me". Despite the transformation in her feelings, 'One And Only' still stands as an upbeat bluesy anthem, bold in its determination to seduce the listener along with the subject of its lyrics. "That song is so happy. It's so sad he's such a knobhead."

"'One And Only' might be your wedding anthem," said one review, picking up on the song's slushy movie origins. "It highlights the most genuine iteration of Adele's voice – conjuring blues and soul giants like Etta James – which belts out the tender lyrics."

Lovesong

The only cover on the album, 'Lovesong' was written by Robert Smith and Simon Gallup, lead singer and bassist respectively of cult British post-punk band, The Cure, a favourite of Adele's mum's. Atypically soft in sentiment as Cure songs go, 'Lovesong' was penned by Smith, so the story goes, for his then fiancée.

Towards the end of her time in Malibu with Rick Rubin, Adele was having a rare bad recording day. The idea that she might cover 'Lovesong' came up, but not from her; perhaps she had discussed the music she grew up listening to in conversation with the musicians around her. Both guitarist Smokey Hormel and Rubin decided Adele might be the woman to resurrect the song. Although worried about her voice which was showing signs of strain after several intensive weeks in the studio, Adele gave it a go. Remarkably given her weariness, the recording that now graces *21* is her first take. Rubin felt it could not be improved upon. And indeed the slightly gravelly quality of Adele's voice suits the intimate and touching sentiments of the song perfectly. While she sang it, the homesick Adele was, she said later, overwhelmed with nostalgia: "It was really weird because I had this kind of 'Christmas Carol' vision of my mum when I was six."

From appearing on the album almost by accident, 'Lovesong' now stands as Adele's tribute to the mother who had so steeped her in music. Penny – initially nervous about the prospect of such a radically different version of a song she knew and loved – was immediately won over by it. "She'd disown me if she didn't like it, but she loved it!" In an interview with *Rolling Stone*, Adele explained what she felt a good cover version should do. "I think it's really important that... you either make it better than the original or you just make it a completely different song."

Slower and considerably more mellow than the original, Adele's version of 'Lovesong' is beautifully arranged. Stripped back instrumentally, it features a pair of classical guitars split across the stereo field right through the song, and strings nestling in with the vocal line which work a treat. Adele later paid tribute to Rubin's work on the production. "It's a really stunning recording... It really is Rick Rubin that song... the sounds... the way it's all miked... Everything."

After a stay of almost five weeks in Malibu's '27 Miles of Scenic Beauty' that had left her feeling homesick, Adele poured into her heartfelt rendition of 'Lovesong' all her longing for home, and the mother who had introduced her to The Cure in the first place. And then she felt better. "It's such a touching song... The whole experience of being in Malibu with Rick Rubin was a bit overwhelming... I felt quite heavy, and that song sort of set me free a little bit."

'Lovesong' continued to transport Adele back to her early North London days. "Whenever I sing this song, I always remember being about five or six and in our tiny flat in Tottenham," she said.

Someone Like You

"It changed my life. And every time I sing it, it changes a little piece of me." And so to 'Someone Like You', the song which puts on naked display the whole landscape of emotion that Adele is capable of bringing to her music. By the time Adele wrote it, she had already written most of the other songs on the album, but was starting to get worried that none of them really touched her personally. "I didn't have that one song that I believed myself on; that one song that moved me. It's important to me that I have that." And then, out of the blue came a sharp stab of news. Adele's ex-boyfriend was to marry someone else.

After the hurt defiance of 'Rolling In The Deep' and 'Rumour Has It'; the later optimism of 'I'll Be Waiting'; and the tender remembrance of 'Lovesong'; 'Someone Like You' plunged Adele into despair at his engagement. "We were so intense I thought we would get married. But that was something he never wanted… So when I found out that he does want that with someone else, it was just the horrible-est feeling ever."

Adele wrote the bones of the song quickly on her acoustic guitar in a fug of emotion at home, and then took it to Dan Wilson. He realised that keeping a tangible sense of how much Adele was hurting was essential. "We didn't try to make it open-ended so it could apply to anybody. We tried to make it as personal as possible." To their first meeting, Adele brought only a few chords and lyrics from the beginning of the song. She and Wilson then "launched in", brainstorming various melodies and lyrics round the piano.

'Someone Like You' was written and recorded in a tiny studio on Santa Monica Boulevard in LA. "It's a place with a high ceiling and a beautiful piano that I love…very simple and unglamorous. I think the space really affected the song and obviously the recording," recalled Wilson. He and Adele decided to keep the production to a minimum, jointly producing the track themselves. "By the end of the second day we had finished a demo which I realised was pretty amazing… And that's what they used on the album."

With instrumental expression coming only through a few subtle variations in tempo and intensity, the result is simplicity itself, pairing Adele's extraordinary vocal with a lone piano; a crack combination which would become familiar from her unforgettable live renditions of the song. "When she sings, there's just the thinnest veil between us and her emotions." said Wilson. "In the room where she's singing, it's pretty hair-raising."

On the face of it, 'Someone Like You' is a pessimistic note on which to end the album, originating as it did in a renewal of the pain of her failed relationship. "When I was writing it, I was feeling pretty miserable and kind of lonely, which contradicts 'Rolling In The Deep', which was, 'I'm going to be fine without you'. This one was me on my knees really. It's so brutally about him." And yet, agonising though it is, 'Someone Like You' is also the song of a woman now able to wish her ex the best, and ready to get on with her life. "The relationship summed up in 'Someone Like You' changed me in a really good way. It's made me who I am at the moment." Though she would continue to get emotional every time she performed it, this moment of catharsis on a cathartic album also represents a bittersweet moment of liberation for Adele. "After I wrote it, I felt more at peace. It set me free."

'Someone Like You' is a triumphant finale which many consider the best thing on the album. "It may be a cliché, but Adele has saved the best until last with this heartfelt and enchanting piano ballad." It is the track of which Adele herself is most proud too. "It's my favourite song that I've ever written, because it's so articulate. It completely sums up how I felt then." It was, she said a song about loss, but hopeful as well as sad. "I don't think I'll ever write a better song than that. I think that'll be my song."

Adele cradles her beloved Louie. And a nice handbag from her extensive collection. BERETTA/SIMS/REX FEATURES

Adele attends a New York Fashion Week show by favoured designer, Barbara Tfank, New York City, September 2009. MIKE COPPOLA/FILMMAGIC

A country girl for once, at the CMT Artists of the Year event, Franklin, Tennessee, November 2010. ED RODE/GETTY IMAGES

Adele in full-flight during the first ever BBC Radio 1 *Live Lounge Special*, Maida Vale Studios, London, January 2011. ANDY SHEPPARD/REDFERNS

Rehearsing for a second appearance on one of her favourite TV shows: *Later… With Jools Holland*, March 2008. ANDRE CSILLAG/REX FEATURES

Singing 'Baby It's You', accompanied by its composer, the legendary Burt Bacharach for the BBC Electric Proms at the Roundhouse, London, October 2008. BRIAN RASIC/REX FEATURES

Taking *21* to America. Adele performs in the studio of California radio station, KCRW, February 2011. LARRY HIRSHOWITZ/CORBIS

Greeting her fans. Adele arrives for *The Late Show With David Letterman* at the Ed Sullivan Theater, New York City, February 2011. GETTY IMAGES

Adele sings 'Someone Like You' in THAT Brit Awards performance, O2 Arena, London, February 2011.

Barclaycard Mercury Prize Nominee for *21*, London,
September 2011. DAVE HOGAN/GETTY IMAGES

'Someone Like You' wows again. On stage at the annual
MTV Video Music Awards, Los Angeles, August 2011.
KEVIN MAZUR/GETTY IMAGES

Red letter day. Adele performing at The Tabernacle in Notting Hill on the day *21* was released in the UK, London, January 2011.
ANDY SHEPPARD/REDFERNS

Every inch the cover girl. On the red carpet at the 2011 MTV Video Music Awards, Los Angeles, August 2011.
JON KOPALOFF/FILMMAGIC

Chapter 7

Hurts So Good

I just wanted to make good songs and I think I've done that.

Adele, 2010

By early autumn 2010, Adele was well and truly out of hiding. Although still officially untitled, her new album was almost ready to roll. And so began a year of performing and promoting the hell out of it, at home and abroad. In September and October, Adele was back in the US, and making a start in New York: "to play a few songs and say, 'Hey, I'm back,'" as Columbia's marketing man, Scott Greer put it.

As part of the wooing process, Adele was to give some small, invitation-only performances to provide industry insiders and VIP guests with a sneak preview of what they could expect from her new record. At one such intimate show at the Largo Theater in Los Angeles, against a red-velvet backdrop and surrounded by vintage lamps, Adele offered up 'Rolling In The Deep', 'Don't You Remember'; 'Turning Tables'; and 'Someone Like You'. "I'm shaking," she said after performing the latter song accompanied, as would become habitual, by a pianist only. "I get upset whenever I sing it." After rounding off the programme with 'Chasing Pavements' and 'Hometown Glory' for good measure, she cried off singing any more, despite the audience clamouring for her to do so. "My voice has been dormant for months, it's pissed off at me for putting it back to work," she said.

Adele's album-blazing promotional tour also took her to Minneapolis and St Paul, where she paid a return visit to the local public radio station, performing unplugged versions of 'Some Like You' and 'Rolling In The Deep' from the new album, along with old favourite 'Chasing Pavements'. In an in-depth interview with the presenters between songs, she revealed, somewhat bashfully, that the new album was to be called *21*. "I was going to call it 'Rolling In The Deep', but that's a bit of a mouthful, and I think it might be a bit like Chinese whispers and turn into something else. Like my drummer thought it was called 'Rolling In The Beep'. And numbers are kind of universal." Asked if she would stay with the number-naming trend for her albums, she said she felt 21 was "the only good-sounding number left: 34's a bit funny, innit?"

On November 1, Adele's blog officially announced the arrival of her new album – and the rationale behind the title. "It's taken a while and it knocked me for six when writing it. It's different from *19*… I deal with things differently now. I'm more patient, more honest, more forgiving and more aware of my own flaws, habits and principles. Something that comes with age I think. So fittingly this record is called *21*… I tried to think of other album titles but couldn't come up with anything that represented the album properly, I kept swerving *21,* thinking it was obvious. But why not be obvious?"

A couple of weeks later, 'Rolling In The Deep' received its first UK airplay on Zane Lowe's Show on Radio 1. That same week, Adele was back to perform on *Later… With Jools Holland*, the show on which she had made her emotional TV debut over three years previously. For *Later…* she sang not 'Rolling In The Deep' but 'Someone Like You' in order to demonstrate what XL MD Ben Beardsworth called "the two sides to the album". Adele's label had originally, he told *Music Week*, been tempted to release *21* in time for Christmas 2010 but elected to wait. "We want to make sure everywhere is set up perfectly to really do the album justice," he added.

Though she had pronounced herself nervous again beforehand,

Adele's performance on *Later…* was simply stunning, and a signal of great things to come. While her debut on that programme had been remarkable, her centred but emotionally charged 2010 performance went down as one of her most memorable. The shy girl, dressed in a floral tunic and perched on a stool, in awe of her fellow guests had been replaced by a fully-fledged diva, copper hair pulled back from her expressive face, her stance strong, her hands expressively punctuating her words.

The album 'set-up' continued with airplay for 'Rolling In The Deep' in the US, and an unveiling on people.com with the stylishly retro black-and-white footage filmed during her stay at the Shangri-La Ranch in Malibu. Though 'Rolling In The Deep' was not destined to be the name of the album, it was to be the first song unleashed from it on a now eagerly awaiting audience. On November 29, it was released as a single in the Netherlands. The week before, Adele had hopped over there to perform it on Dutch TV on the *MaDiWoDoVrijdag Show,* which got the song's first TV airing.

In a winningly camp interview with presenter Paul de Leeuw, she reiterated that *21* reflected the fact that she was more aware of her flaws than before. "I used to think I was the greatest girlfriend in the world. And I'm really not." There was also a little tribute to her beloved Louie. "No one's ever going to love me as much as he loves me." And Adele was cock-a-hoop when the presenters sprang a surprise and presented her with a Dutch bike live on the show, complete with bell, and a big red bow and pennant flag on the back. Her only worry, she said, was that she had already asked for a bike from her mum for Christmas.

The following day, 'Rolling In The Deep' was released as a single in the US. Adele went back to the West Coast a few days later to perform the song on the *Ellen DeGeneres Show,* but she also had another exciting booking on this latest US trip. She had been asked to perform as part of Country Music Television's Artists of the Year Special in Nashville, an extravagantly presented annual celebration honouring the achievements of country music stars. One of the acts to be fêted that year was Lady Antebellum. A couple of months before, when she was promoting her new album in LA, Adele found time to go to a gig by the hit Nashville three-piece, after getting heavily into their music while touring the US the previous year. During her stay at the Shangri-La Ranch in Malibu, the band's song 'Need You Now' had saturated the airwaves, cementing her fondness for their lovelorn country ballads.

At the CMT special on December 3, Adele was to perform a cover of that very song in tribute to the band, in a duet with R&B singer-turned-country music star, Darius Rucker. Adele looked right at home, and her high-profile appearance in the spiritual heartland of country music set the seal on a year in which the genre had become increasingly important to her. Her version of 'Need You Now', sung with Rucker, was later released on a limited edition CD of *21*.

From a performance for country music royalty, to a performance for proper British royalty. Adele was back home in time to put in an appearance at the Royal Variety Performance at the London Palladium on December 9. An excited Adele ("always watched it, always loved it") sang 'Rolling In The Deep' in front of a rather rattled Charles and Camilla, whose car had been attacked by rioting students on the way to the theatre. She found it nerve-racking performing at what she called "such an iconic British institution", a situation not helped by head-butting the mike when she walked on. "Luckily it was a wide shot," she said. "I was scared my nose was going to start bleeding. And then I winked at Camilla."

Adele then had a bit of a ball, hobnobbing with her fellow stars. "Got to meet Susan Boyle, who was delightful and seriously the sweetest person I have ever met. Also got to meet Dappy from N-Dubz, who is an absolute gent; Michael McIntyre [who] hosted – he's funnier in real life than when he's doing stand-up – and Robbie Williams!" she reported later on her blog. Only with the Robbie encounter did she revert to her previous star-struck type, remarking, "I won't dare go into that because I might shit myself out of excitement if I re-live the moment!"

Just in case any fans were starting to think that it was all going to her head, Adele then brought things down to earth in typically self-deprecating style. "It was a very glamorous affair until me and Paloma Faith, who I've known for years, knocked it down a peg when we ordered some chicken nuggets and drank cheap red wine in the hotel next door!"

In mid-December, Adele headed off on her first visit to Japan, in advance of the pre-Christmas release of 'Rolling In The Deep' there. It turned out to be something of a wasted trip as Adele went down with the flu and was unable to fulfil most of the promotional turns that had been set up for her. By the time Christmas arrived, however, she was able to take a brief but much-needed break at home in London, happy in the knowledge that, after all her hard work on the road, everything was falling nicely into place for the January release of her album.

In the run-up to Christmas there was also the unexpected bonus of seeing an old favourite – her cover version of 'Make You Feel My Love' – riding high in the UK charts after it had been sung twice during the seventh series of *The X Factor*. After a stirring rendition by eventual series runner-up, Rebecca Ferguson, at the beginning of November, Adele's version of the song had risen to number four in the charts, over 20 places higher than when she originally released it as a single.

It was a family Christmas. Adele's highlights were "the blueberry crunch cake I made and the ship-in-a-bottle kit I got from my nan". Then, with the release of *21* less than a month away, it was back to work. Accompanied by Louie, she headed north for some radio interviews, and performed a memorable set at Smooth Radio's Love Live Music event on January 5, in the intimate surroundings of the Cavern Club in Liverpool. "I might sound a bit like Tom Waits meets Tina Turner because I've got the back-end of bronchitis," she announced to the packed crowd on taking to the stage, all in black, and with minimal make-up. Adele later acknowledged the thrill of performing at the historic venue: "It sent chills down my spine! And the brick work on the original Cavern Club over the road with all the names engraved of who's played there made me dribble!" But enjoyable as the trip was, it was just the start of a whole series of performances that would belie the underlying state of her voice.

There was also an early warning sign of the extent to which the press would follow her every move during 2011, and not just her musical ones. During an interview with XFM Manchester, for whom she also put on another intimate gig in early January, Adele sounded off about an interview published in that morning's issue of *The Sun*. "They've written this piece on me saying 'New Album, New Fella' and that I want to get engaged this year. I told them that so tongue-in-cheek, like a fake New Year's resolution. And now they're making out I've got some new fella."

'Rolling In The Deep' was released as a single in the UK on January 17. It easily beat off competition from Britney Spears' comeback single, 'Hold It Against Me', but couldn't quite overtake Bruno Mars' 'Grenade' to provide Adele with her first number one single the following weekend. Still, it meant that listeners all over the country were thrilling to the new single, and the power of Adele's voice. The voice itself was at home, however, having been ordered to rest in silence, and keep off the booze and fags. Adele was again feeling the after-effects of her December bout of flu. But there were some terrific reviews of 'Rolling In The Deep' to cheer her.

"Right now it's damp and cold and Adele sounds like warm Ribena and horns," quipped an impressed Morwenna Ferrier in *The Guardian*, designating 'Rolling In The Deep' her pick of the week's single releases.

"Best of all, for once, the production is all behind her, emerging in a fan formation like a street gang, ready for a fight. The ghostly harmonies, the propulsive hand-claps, the played-with-my-face piano... it's all there to support that remarkable voice in full flight. And it flies, like, really really high," blogged Fraser McAlpine on the BBC Radio 1 website.

"If we were the wrong-un who inspired this pop-soul colossus, we'd be feeling a mixture of fear, shame and regret. A hell of a lot of regret," concluded *Digital Spy*, awarding the single five stars.

Amid all the excitement, Adele asked her fans to spare a thought for her idol Etta James who had just been diagnosed with leukaemia and dementia. Posting some of Etta's favourite performances on her blog, she wrote, "I just cried and laughed at the same time watching them back again. She is so incredible, no one's got nothing on her. A little piece of me dies and goes to heaven every single time I hear her."

Adele's new album had its UK release on January 24. It also went on sale the same day in Australia, Austria, Germany, Ireland, the Netherlands, Switzerland, Poland and France. A revived Adele celebrated with another intimate gig, this time at The Tabernacle in London's Notting Hill. It was another bravura outing. With *21* finally out there, both in record shops and in cyberspace, her real live performance prompted one blogger to the "less than revolutionary thought that the only thing that should divide the artist and the performer is the performance itself. Everything else is balls... Adele feels like an opened window on the sweaty bus of popular music. There's no artifice, no bullshit and little trace of ambition. Adele just does what she does, but she does it better than anyone else. And that's all we need right now."

There was, of course, no sign that the impending global album release was going to her head. Adele was on top chatty form. Her audience learned that there were little bits of her acrylic nails stuck in her guitar; that she had stalked Kevin Costner at the CMT Awards; and that she loved Leona Lewis so much that she had spent close on £100 voting for her when she was on *The X Factor*. Adele enjoyed performing live back in her hometown immensely, blogging the next day: "It was so incredible to play at home again. I realised this morning my last show here was Christmas 2008! That's illegal in my books! I had such a brilliant time. I was nervous, excited, teary but over the moon!"

The Monday night Tabernacle gig, streamed live on Adele's website, was only the beginning of an extraordinary week. By Wednesday, it became clear that *21* had gone down a storm both across Europe and beyond, having gone straight to the top of the download charts in countries such as France, Austria, Germany and Australia. Midweek, there was a flying visit to Paris for a TV appearance before heading back on the last Eurostar of the night. In true superstar style, a police escort was provided to make sure she caught it. "I felt like Whitney Houston meets Obama," she said.

The following morning, Adele did her third Live Lounge session for BBC Radio 1 at the Maida Vale Studios, performing six songs in a specially extended, first ever *Live Lounge* Special. There were three from the new album: 'Rolling In The Deep', 'Someone Like You' and 'Don't You Remember' plus 'Hometown Glory' and 'Chasing Pavements'. The sixth song was a cover of Cheryl Cole's 'Promise This', chosen and performed by Adele specially for the session. Adele, who had recently met Cole at the Royal Variety Performance said she was "extra nervous" about doing the song because "I love her so much. She's my favourite person ever." When a text came in from a listener after the performance, saying how much she liked her laugh – Adele had been on cackling fine form during an interview with Fearne Cotton beforehand – Adele revealed that her voice doctor had told her not to laugh any more. "Isn't that depressing? Laughing's my life!"

The next day, Adele was on British TV for a change, performing 'Rolling In The Deep' on *This Morning*, and chatting to presenters Eamonn Holmes and Ruth Langsford on the sofa. When asked about the ex she had to thank for the album, Adele said, "It went sour, but he was actually wonderful. I'm actually at peace with it now, especially now the album's out and I'm not so uptight about it any more." Being Adele, however, she couldn't leave things on a poignant note. She caused great hilarity by adding: "I know you're probably watching because I know you're probably really jealous that you're not with me any more," and then rocked with loud cackles of laughter. "I'm joking. No, really, we spoke the other day and I'm at peace with it now." Later that day she finally took possession of her new bike, the one that she had acquired from her friends on Dutch TV. She posted a photograph on her website of herself riding it, all smiles, the big red bow now festooning the handlebars.

The freewheeling smiles could also have had something to do with the largely rapturous reviews of *21* beaming from the pages of the national press. "A progressive, grown-up second collection, it ought to ensure Adele is around for 23, 25, 27 and beyond, " said *The Guardian,* in a four-star review. "Where previously her slight, observational songs seemed barely able to carry her powerful voice, the emotional and musical heft of these styles enables her to really spread her vocal wings," said the *Daily Telegraph*. "Hers is a voice that seems to go right to your heart." "It really is so marvellous, you're almost compelled to stand up and applaud it after the first listen," agreed BBC Music. "Every track is a highlight. *21* is simply stunning." MSN Music said: "*21* contains a vocal performance that places Adele in the league of the true greats. She's a soul diva in the best sense."

One of the few notes of dissent came from *The Observer* reviewer Kitty Empire, who loved 'Someone Like You' but felt let down by much of the rest: "… more of this bunny-boiling intensity wouldn't go amiss on an album where the shivers don't come as often as they should".

On Sunday, January 30 however, there were more than shivers of excitement at the news that *21* had gone straight in at number one on the UK album charts. And it had done it by notching up a phenomenal number of sales: 208,090, the highest January first week's sale since Adele's bugbear band, The Arctic Monkeys, had released *Whatever People Say I Am, That's What I'm Not* in 2006. Her first album, *19*, had also re-entered the charts at number four.

By the middle of the following week, *21* was also the bestselling album in Austria, Belgium, Germany, Ireland, the Netherlands, New Zealand and Switzerland, and was riding high in the top five in Denmark, Norway, Australia and France. Adele was both astonished and delighted. But there was precious little time to bask in the hometown – and continental – glory of having a number one album. Adele was already back in the US, ready for another frenetic round of interviews and appearances ahead of the North American release of *21* on February 22.

On February 2 she blogged from New York: "It's freezing, there's snow everywhere, but it's lovely to be back!… (*Also* two weeks today since I had a cigarette! God I want one to celebrate, but I'm going to stay strong!)" Adele was clearly trying hard to put her voice first. She was also already missing Louie, particularly when she saw the sweet photograph of her cuddling him in the new issue of US magazine *Nylon*. She did a short promotional tour which took her to Washington DC ahead of tickets going on sale for her forthcoming North American tour in May. Then it was home to perform at the 2011 Brit Awards on February 15.

The nerves were jangling even more than usual when Adele learnt she was down to sing after Take That and before Rihanna in the running order. "All day I was thinking, this is gonna be a disaster," she said later. Even after a performance so emotionally redolent that she reduced herself – and a sizeable chunk of the audience – to tears, Adele didn't feel much better about things. "I thought it was fucking shit actually!" she told *Q* magazine. "It was so flat at the end, obviously because I started crying. Last time I was at the Brits I was with my boyfriend who the song's about. And then the audience, my peers, stood up. I was so emotional. I got back to my dressing room on my hands and knees..."

With her unerring sense of occasion, and her ability to come up with something special despite petrifying stage fright, this was, perhaps, Adele's seminal performance among so many memorable ones. It was the saddest of songs so beautifully, fragilely true in its rendition that millions carried on talking about it, long after the final notes had died away. She had, in the words of numerous headline writers the following day, stolen the show. Clashmusic.com called it "a true 'Where were you?' moment... Adele's performance has managed to arguably outstrip the awards themselves".

The effect on sales was phenomenal too. 'Someone Like You', released as a single alongside *21,* shot up from below the Top 40 to number one, while 'Rolling In The Deep' rose to number four. With *21* still at number one in the album charts, this famously made Adele the first artist since The Beatles in 1964 to achieve top five hits in both the singles and the album charts in a single week. "Sometimes the stars just align for you," was how Jonathan Dickins put it.

But once again, there was no time to sit taking in those stars. With *21* due out in the US and Canada in less than a week, it was across the Atlantic again for another round of interviews and TV appearances, including *The Today Show* and *The Late Show With David Letterman* in New York; and *The Ellen DeGeneres Show* in Los Angeles. There was also a six-song unplugged set for VH1, recorded in Harlem the previous month, and including a glorious cover of '(You Make Me Feel Like A) Natural Woman'.

It was all about reminding a nation of that British two-time Grammy winner who made everyone sit up when she popped onto *Saturday Night Live* in front of 15 million people, and, well, stole the show. Fast forward a year and a bit, and there were the inevitable questions about what, or who, had inspired the songs on the new album. It would have been hard to be venomous on American prime-time television, of course, but there were signs perhaps that Adele was mellowing towards her ex. "I'm less bitter. Especially now the record's out and doing well," she said in one interview. Almost a year on, and some sort of healing process was occasionally taking over from the heartbreak. "I am absolutely speechless. I didn't know what to do with myself when I found out 'Someone Like You' was number one [in the UK]!" blogged Adele from the US before her *Letterman* appearance. "That song is so special to me and it's even more so now, thank you so much. And who the hell is still buying the album at home?... The album's out here tomorrow too, I'm shitting myself."

Adele's *Letterman* appearance aired on the eve of her album's release. Adele performed 'Rolling In The Deep', with her team off-set, willing her not to say the word 'shit' in the lyrics to the opening verse on prime-time TV. The normally cuss-happy Adele passed the test, substituting the less offensive – although far less effective – 'stuff'. Letterman was impressed. "Woah, man... Adele, *21*... Fantastic... That was beautiful... Come back anytime."

The US reviews of *21* were broadly welcoming of what was inevitably being referred to stateside as her "sophomore" album. "Now that she's legal... Adele has toughened her tone, trimmed the jazz frippery and sounds ready for a pub fight," said *Rolling Stone*."At its best, *21* is that rarest pop commodity: timeless," was the verdict of *Entertainment Weekly*. *The LA Times* thought that, "Overall, *21* shows that Adele, now 22, is towering in the same landscape where some of her contemporaries, beehived or not, have lost all their bearings." And *The Washington Post:* "Her sophomore disc, the-even better *21,* is a break-up album with strings and a vague inclination toward rootsiness. Everything on it is precisely calibrated to transcend genres, to withstand trends, to be just so."

The public response to the new album was, however, overwhelming: *21* went straight in at number one on the *Billboard* 200, having shifted 352,000 copies in its first week on sale. Even before it was released in the US by iTunes, it was already in the Top 10 on the basis of pre-sales. On its release, it went straight to number one on the digital charts too.

And *19* had seen a big resurgence, re-entering the Top 20 at number 16. After the coast-to-coast gigs, the months on the road far from home, the endless TV and radio interviews, Adele had finally conquered America. *The Independent*, observing her success from the other side of the pond, commented that the "rootsy sound" of *21* was enough to "persuade a growing number of Americans that this bonhomous Brit is very much the real deal".

"Nothing that's happened to me over the last month at home or abroad has sunk in, because I was so frightened of releasing it that I grew concrete skin. But it definitely just cracked!" So ran Adele's blog on March 7, reflecting on her US number one, just before heading back to the UK, where *21* remained at number one too. Adele was to have a couple of weeks break, before setting off on the European and UK stages of her mammoth Adele Live tour in support of *21*. It should have been a chance to relax and revel in the reception that her music was getting. But instead, the events of the past few months, which had raised her right up the celebrity stakes in parallel with her soaring chart positions, also brought some of the more unsavoury aspects of fame. That concrete skin would have helped with some of what was to follow.

First, her dad sold his story to *The Sun*. Under the headline, "I was an alcoholic and rotten dad to Adele. It tears me up inside," Mark Evans described his chequered relationship with Adele since he split up with her mother, and his battle with the bottle following the death of his father. He claimed that the music he played when she was a small child had influenced his daughter, although he found listening to her own music too upsetting because he "couldn't bear the memories it brought up". But after some years of estrangement, he and Adele, he said, were now getting on great, "... so who knows, one of these days I might even find the courage to see one of her shows".

Adele was mortified. "He has no fucking right to talk about me... He gave them private childhood photographs. I was pissed off: we've no relationship," she said to *Rolling Stone*. The following day, *The Sun* published another story that horrified her: "Teenage mum, cramped flats and truancy... the truth behind Adele's brave struggle to stardom." This time, the piece purported to quote Adele's much-loved gran,

Doreen "who proudly showed us a photo of Adele she keeps in her bus pass wallet and said: 'She is just the same but we don't see much of her just because she's so busy. I haven't seen her for a year.'"

"Oh my God, my fucking *nan?* They're vicious." Adele told *Rolling Stone* that a reporter from *The Sun* had ambushed her gran for an interview at a bus stop; and *Q* magazine that they had made the story up. Nevertheless, Adele was so upset by the exposure of her jealously guarded private life that she started smoking again.

Once an avid reader of the gossip mags, Adele was having to come to terms with the fact that she was now appearing in them almost weekly. "I fucking hate being in them." Regularly followed and papped, no aspect of her life seemed safe from media scrutiny. She told *Q* that she employed a security guard, and was convinced her mobile phone was being tapped. And she no longer felt at ease in restaurants: "You've got to be careful what you say." There were weird fans too, like the camera-wielding one in Cologne who didn't know when to back off. And the one who sent her a "crispy" tissue in the mail. "There was a note saying, 'This is what I imagine you doing to me.' Oh, you sent me a crispy tissue. I'll definitely get in touch with you. Hey, let's get married and have children!"

Adele may have laughed it off, but after that she started having her mail screened. There were still lots of inspiring letters among the more disturbing ones. "I get a lot of mail from people who tell me that I make them really happy to be themselves, and really comfortable with who they are, which I love," she said.

In the space of a month through March and April, Adele's tour took her from Oslo in Norway, to Sweden, Germany, Italy, Spain, France, Belgium, the Netherlands, Denmark and Ireland, before ending with a week of gigs back in the UK. Many of the dates were upgraded to bigger venues due to public demand for tickets. Louie went with her, and there were plenty of highlights, despite how bewildering her onstage banter must often have seemed to European audience members with only language-school English. In Brussels, a school-aged gay lad even thanked her for giving him the courage to come out ("I had to leave so I didn't burst into tears", said Adele later).

In the crowd at her final gig at the Shepherds Bush Empire on April 21, celebrity friends like Mark Ronson, James Corden and Alan Carr were there to welcome her back to her hometown. Christa D'Souza, who was soon to interview Adele for UK *Vogue* was also there, later writing: "On she half-totters, half-runs, in a sparkly black brocade dress, her ginger-biscuit hair pinned back in Beyoncé-style ringlets. Theatrically she fans her creamy, ample bosom, then jumps up and down, clenching and unclenching doll-like fists to indicate that, for her too, this is an awfully big moment." Even after a month on tour, singing the same songs, night after night; Adele was still having plenty of those moments. In Birmingham, a few days before, she had been moved to tears on stage as the crowd sang along to 'Make You Feel My Love', and for a long moment, she couldn't go on. "I was home, I'm so patriotic, I was so emotional," she later said of that night.

Digging deep emotionally to give this calibre of performance night after night was taking a toll, however, and Adele gave two interviews during the European leg of her tour which revealed that fact. In late March she spoke to *Rolling Stone* in Hamburg. The interview describes her as being "a bit out of sorts", drinking red wine and smoking more than the seven cigarettes she claimed she was allowing herself per day. Later, before going on stage for that evening's concert, she told the interviewer: "I have the shakes... I'm scared of audiences... I've just got to bear it. But I don't like touring. I have anxiety attacks a lot."

In Copenhagen, a couple of weeks later, she was interviewed for *Q*. She told Sylvia Patterson that the previous night she had been doing what she increasingly did on tour "when I'm having a bit of a wobbly", sitting up until 5 a.m. in her hotel room, alone with Louie and a bottle of red wine, Skyping her friends back home, and feeling homesick. "The more successful I get, the more insecurities I'm getting, it's weird," she said. "Not bad ones or nothing. Just about who I am. How I feel about things. I don't know if it's because I'm so blown away that people like what I do, but I just feel like I'm never going to live up to it."

Adele also got into trouble after apparently complaining in the same interview about the amount of income tax she was now being required to pay. "I'm mortified I have to pay 50%! Cos I'd be sitting there for five hours if me appendix burst or something; the trains are always late; most state schools are *fucking* shit and I've gotta give you like four million quid? Are you *fucking* having a laugh?" When the interview came out at the end of May, there was something of a Twitter backlash. A blogger for *Guardian Music* said it was "upsetting to hear this musician I admire seem as greedy as the most moat-friendly, port-stained Tory grandee", and pointed out that The Beatles had had to pay 95%. For once, Adele and her big mouth had said something less than endearing.

At least the more patriotically British Adele was looking forward to the wedding of Prince William and Catherine Middleton at the end of April, when she was due to have three weeks off. There'd be a barbecue party; and perhaps she'd even get some Union Jack ghetto nails done, she said. Then soon afterwards, it would be off to America to launch her Adele Live tour there. Perhaps, in the light of her comments in Copenhagen, the thought of such a huge tour, and another long stretch away from home so soon were concerning her. In the event, she was home much sooner than anyone could have anticipated.

Chapter 8

Little Voice

Didn't I give it all? / Tried my best
Gave you everything I had / Everything, and no less

Adele, 'Take It All'

By March 2011, the music world was at Adele's feet. Her critically acclaimed second album, *21*, released in January, had debuted at number one in the UK, the US and in 17 other countries across Europe. Her astounding rendition of 'Someone Like You' at the 2011 Brit Awards had led to more than 5.5 million hits on YouTube for the uploaded performance. Her glamorous, diva look was putting her on glossy magazine covers. But the way she sounded was faltering.

Adele's voice problems first became apparent at the beginning of 2011. After her bout of flu the previous December, her voice failed to regain its full strength. Despite a Brits performance that gave the ultimate lie to anything being wrong, Adele's voice was in fact getting "weaker and weaker until it eventually broke... I didn't realise at the time, because I'd never had anything wrong with my voice, ever. But I'd also never sung as much." Later, in an interview on *The Graham Norton Show*, she said that the problem stemmed from a radio show she had done in Paris the week before *21* was released. "They couldn't do sound for shit, so I had to scream over the band, and my voice just went."

A miserable ban from caffeine, cigarettes and alcohol followed. "I'm not smoking, I'm not drinking alcohol. No caffeine, no fizzy drinks, no curry... [I] can only chew mints, can't suck mints..." For a Coke, red-wine and ciggy-loving girl, the ban represented a catalogue of misery. Having to give up the fags was the worst of it. "I hate it. I really want to smoke. I love it; it's my thing," she lamented. She did admit later that she had noticed an improvement, despite quipping flippantly that she would "rather my voice be a bit shit so I can have a fucking laugh". An equally difficult ban on talking was also imposed. "I had to sit in silence for nine days, chalkboard round my neck....like a kid in the naughty corner. Like a Victorian mute."

The regime worked, her voice returned, and her 20-date tour of Europe and the UK went ahead as planned through March and April. But it was a temporary respite. May brought further rumbles of trouble ahead. Returning to the US once more, Adele appeared on the results show for *Dancing With The Stars,* and delivered a full-throttle rendition of 'Rolling In The Deep'. But she was unable to sing her planned second song, a cover of '(You Make Me Feel Like A) Natural Woman', explaining to the show's host that she couldn't hit the high notes it required because her voice was "knackered". The *Daily Mail* ran pap pictures of her out on the town in Beverly Hills the previous night with Tinie Tempah, clutching a packet of fags. "Has American success cost Adele her voice... or is it just the cigarettes?" ran the headline.

Then: crisis. In the last week of May and halfway through her US tour, she was in Minneapolis, set to play the city's Ogden Theater. During a morning Skype call on the day of her show, her voice "suddenly switched off like a light". It was she said, "As if someone pulled a curtain over my throat. I knew something was wrong and panicked but convinced myself I'd be fine." By the time she got to her soundcheck for the evening show, it was clear that she wouldn't be able to perform, and on medical advice the show was cancelled.

Adele insisted on travelling to Denver, Colorado for her next concert two days later. It went ahead, despite her private qualms that it was the wrong thing to do. Her worst fears were realised when, during the show she felt something "ripping" in her throat. Adrenalin kicked in, and she managed to finish her set. In the wake of her Minneapolis cancellation, the Denver audience, some of whom had paid 10 times face value for tickets that had been sold out months before, was ecstatic that the concert had gone ahead as planned. Under the headline "Despite Laryngitis, Adele Gives a Powerhouse Concert that Does Not Disappoint", one reviewer wrote that "from the moment Adele stepped out on the stage, it was clear that she was planning on giving a full performance, starting with the stirring 'Hometown Glory' that showed no sign of weakness." The only time she showed any sign of being below par he said was during 'Take It All' where "for about a minute in the middle of the song she looked genuinely pained". Even as she introduced the song, Adele asked the audience to help her out in singing it, because she said, there were some notes in it that my voice "just ain't going to get".

It was all too plain that Adele's voice problems were more serious than a simple bout of laryngitis. The following week's shows were cancelled and she flew to Los Angeles to rest, still hoping to resume her tour in San Francisco on June 4. An otolaryngology specialist in LA soon put paid to that. Adele was diagnosed with a haemorrhage of the vocal cords and told that a month's absolute voice rest was imperative. The remaining dates of her US tour had to be cancelled. In a press release, Adele commented, "I'm really frustrated. I was hoping with a week's rest I'd be better to sing again straight away. However there is absolutely nothing I can do but take the doctor's advice and rest some more. I'm so sorry. See you soon, love Adele."

Devastated at having to cut short a tour she seemed to be enjoying – "I met so many amazing people and got to play with the best artists I've ever played alongside" – Adele flew home to London. Enforced rest was not a prescription she submitted to easily. She blogged on June 21 that she was filling her time "watching box sets and sorting things out into neat piles", and also trying to get back into cooking. There was one exciting night out at a select, invitation-only, celebrity-studded gig given by Beyoncé at Shepherds Bush Empire, and there were reports in some quarters that Adele had been "gutted" at having to turn down the chance to duet with Beyoncé on stage at Glastonbury a few days before. Rumours were also circulating that she had had lunch with Jay-Z to discuss a future collaboration. "Adele to be Jay-Zing Pavements" was *The Sun*'s headline. Whatever the truth of both matters, while recuperating back at home, Adele listened to Beyoncé's music for hours, and started the task of uploading over a thousand CDs to her iTunes account. She was, however, "bored stiff".

Despite her frustration, the layoff seemed to do the trick. The condition of her voice improved, and by early July Adele had recovered enough to appear at Heaven in London for Pride weekend, followed a few days later by a gig at London's Roundhouse for the iTunes Festival, appropriately enough given the uploading that had kept her busy during her month of enforced rest. It was a triumphant hometown return. "Nothing gives me more pleasure than being at home and singing to you guys," she told the 2,000-strong capacity Roundhouse crowd, who moved her almost to tears by singing along en masse to her final number, 'Someone Like You'. Immediately afterwards, Adele was trending number one on Twitter, and the reviews would be glowing. "When she sang she swooped back up to an elite plateau, where just a voice and a piano can bring tears to the eyes," wrote the London *Evening Standard*. And her voice held up well. "If there are residual cracks in Adele's pipes, you can't hear them: the word 'hometown' easily wraps itself around the venue's lofting ironwork," said *The Observer*.

Later that month, Adele pronounced herself "unbelievably chuffed" to have been shortlisted when the nominees for the 2011 Mercury Prize for Album of the Year were announced. Adele's *21* was installed as second favourite by the bookies, behind PJ Harvey's *Let England Shake*. A few days later, there was further excitement with the news of seven nominations for her 'Rolling In The Deep' video at the 2011 MTV Music Video Awards – the VMAs – including one for Video of the Year. "Flabbergasted about the VMA nominations!" she posted on her blog, accompanied by a glamorous and cheerful photograph of herself in big sunglasses, seated in a leather armchair. "I'm thinking about releasing a range of chairs to celebrate," she quipped, in a reference to the video which features a sitting-down Adele.

Then came the sad news of the death of Amy Winehouse. Adele blogged her own tribute to Winehouse under the heading "Amy Flies in Paradise". "Not many people have it in them to do something they love, simply because they love it," she wrote. "We believed every word she wrote, and it would sink in deep when she sang them. Amy paved the way for artists like me and made people excited about British music again... I don't think she ever realised just how brilliant she was and how important she is, but that just makes her even more charming." It must have been hard for Adele not to recall all those times she herself had been compared to Winehouse, whose fragility had, in the end, got the better of her talent. Though made of sterner stuff, Adele's own recent troubles were a stark reminder of just how vulnerable the whole damn business could make you.

When she resumed her 'Adele Live' tour on August 9 with a rescheduled concert at the Orpheum Theatre in Vancouver, Adele dedicated 'Make You Feel My Love' to Winehouse, a gesture she would make part of her show over the following week. And with London in the grip of the summer riots on the night of her Vancouver opener, she prefaced 'Hometown Glory' by saying: "I have to sing this one for my hometown. London is under attack by a bunch of idiots."

From Vancouver, it was down the west coast via Seattle, Los Angeles and San Diego, before a final run of rescheduled gigs in Las Vegas, Salt Lake City and St Paul. Most had sold out within minutes. "Attending an Adele concert is like going to mass at the Church of Soul. Adele, the prophet of bluesy truth, presides," wrote a reviewer who attended her Seattle concert. He looked around the audience as she sang 'Someone Like You', and "saw people crying, others swaying from side to side with their eyes closed and hands in the air. Now was the time to testify, it would seem. And she gave us all that chance, that outlet, that sweet confession as she turned the mic towards the audience and said, 'Now, you sing.' And we did. In sweet harmony, the army of Adele sang out."

Adele's two Los Angeles concerts were a scorching hot ticket. Her first show at the Greek Theater was attended by *Twilight* star Robert Pattinson and Jessica Simpson. Two nights later, at the Hollywood Palladium, Ryan O'Neal, Dita von Teese, Dwight Yoakam and blogger Perez Hilton were all in the crowd, as was Rick Rubin. "You might have thought the Grateful Dead was in town, what with all the desperate-looking music fans crowding Sunset Boulevard on the hunt for a miracle ticket," wrote *The Hollywood Reporter*.

The 2011 VMAs ceremony took place in Los Angeles on August 28. It was a crazy, hype-steeped occasion, full of theatrics as the line-up of A-list artists vied with each other to be the story of the night. Beyoncé announced just before the show that she was pregnant. Lady Gaga appeared in drag and attempted to kiss Britney Spears. Chris Brown flew high into the air. Bruno Mars performed an Amy Winehouse tribute. Katy Perry sang 'Teenage Dreams' accompanied by a Technicolor catwalk show by scantily clad models, and won Video of the Year for 'Firework'. And Adele, whose video for 'Rolling In The Deep' won four of the seven awards for which it had been nominated, chose to sing 'Someone Like You', clad in black and accompanied by her lone piano player. A few days later, she told Jonathan Ross that she had felt "pretty out of place" and had wished she was "at home with my girlfriends".

Still, despite Beyoncé's rubbing of her baby bump, and Lady Gaga's alter-ego antics, Adele's was the performance of the night for many. "So what was her gimmick? Standing in one spot in an elegant dress and belting the heck out of her song 'Someone Like You'. That was it. And it was precisely that simple, classy approach that earned her a standing ovation from the crowd and offered further proof that she is one of the most universally embraceable artists in contemporary pop music," was the verdict from *The Washington Post*.

But then the trouble began again. Adele arrived back in London at the end of August suffering from a cold. "Just got home, so tired," she blogged. With another run of UK shows set to begin on September 4, there was little time to rest however: it was relentless. On September 3 she appeared on the much-anticipated first episode of Jonathan Ross' 'comeback' ITV chat show. Ross, chasing viewer approval as well as ratings after his departure from the BBC, could not have plucked from the firmament a more luminous star than hers with which to attempt to re-gild his career.

Looking coolly elegant in a simple, sixties-style spangle-trimmed black frock, and a striking, backcombed hairdo, Adele topped the bill, following Hollywood A-lister Sarah Jessica Parker and Formula 1 ace Lewis Hamilton onto the sofa, and considerately telling Ross that she had a cold as he greeted her with a kiss. In conversation, she was her usual, ebullient self, and there was much cackling laughter. Yes, she got into trouble for not playing bigger venues. No she was not a massive fan of touring, and US audiences were "pretty crazy". Yes, she was single – "I'm always single: it's really hard to meet someone". Of her most recent boyfriend she remarked with trademark candour: "No way is he getting a song about him. He would ride that wave for ever. That's how much of a dickhead he is." Adele also let slip to Ross – and 4.3 million viewers – about her supposedly hush-hush next studio project. "I'm doing a theme," she said, whereupon Ross began to sing the James Bond tune. During the laughter that ensued, Adele – tellingly – reached up to feel the glands in her neck.

The banter and indiscretions over, Adele stood up to sing. Her performance of 'Turning Tables" was a little throaty but as beautifully soulful and centred as ever. As the credits rolled, even the ITV continuity announcer couldn't contain himself. "She's amazing," he purred. The next day was a different story. Adele was forced to cancel the first two gigs of her impending 15–date UK tour in Plymouth and Bournemouth. "I'm as useless as a slug right now. I've had a rotten cold since I got home earlier this week and was hoping it wouldn't make its way onto my chest. But unfortunately it has, and it's leaving me breathless and I can't hold any of my notes when I sing," she blogged.

On September 6, Adele attended the Mercury Prize ceremony at London's Grosvenor House Hotel, but did not sing live as she had been scheduled to do. She joined Jools Holland on stage for a brief chat, telling everyone that she was "fucking gutted" not to be singing, but otherwise kept a low profile. On the night, *21* lost out to PJ Harvey's *Let England Shake*, a result generally welcomed in the industry given Adele's already stratospheric sales.

The following day, Adele pulled out of her scheduled concert in Cardiff with hours to go, and cancelled her next gig in Blackpool. On her blog she posted a photograph of herself, pale and un–made-up, holding up a note reading, 'I'm so sorry'. "I woke up feeling a bit better, but not by a lot, but decided to head towards Cardiff anyway in the hope I'd be able to sing tonight. Halfway there I realised it was unrealistic, and so have come back home to rest." She was breathless, she said, and her chest was "disgusting". At the time, Adele was still putting her illness down to a cold that had turned into a chest infection, and not to her previous voice problems. "This has nothing to do with my throat before. I'm sure lots of you feel like this as well, it's going round," she tried to reassure fans. Two more gigs in Wolverhampton were also cancelled before Adele – "stuffed full of antibiotics" and a little rested – was able to start the tour with a concert at the De Montfort Hall in Leicester on September 13. There was no evidence that she was operating on reduced power. "Thank God I'm fucking well, I've been ill as a dog!" she told the audience. The *Daily Telegraph* awarded her performance five stars. The following eight gigs went ahead as planned, taking Adele to Newcastle, Manchester, London – including a one-night-only concert at the Royal Albert Hall, later released on DVD – Edinburgh and Glasgow, and winning widespread praise and adulation. "Every note was clear and powerful," was a typical comment.

Once again, because of her sheer determination to continue, Adele's live performances belied the real state of her health. The physical cost not only of completing the tour, but of giving her audiences her all was soon all-too evident however. With a 10-date US tour of already rescheduled US shows due to start in Atlantic City on October 7, Adele's voice "switched off" again, "mid-conversation". A second haemorrhage on her vocal cords was diagnosed, and the whole US tour had to be cancelled.

Adele's disappointment and anguish is almost palpable in her 'Important Blog' post of October 4. Pointedly, she blames her problems on her punishing touring schedule: "The fact is, I have never been able to fully recover from any of the problems that I've had, and then continue to rest even once I'm recovered, because of my touring commitments. I've been offered the chance to not tour at all to save anything like this from happening again, but I simply hate letting you down. Although now I'm having to let you down once again, through no fault of my own really."

Adele was quick to try and quell suggestions that her smoking had played a part in her condition. She had, she said, done everything the doctor ordered to try and alleviate her problems, however bitter a pill it might have been to swallow. "I stuck to a strict regime of numerous diets, steaming, vocal rest and vocal warm ups. Which is very necessary but insanely grim," she blogged on October 4. Her frequent comments in the past about how much she loved smoking, and her denial that the habit might have any harmful effect on her voice, did seem like madness given what she was now going through. "Smoking is not the reason I got laryngitis – it was because I was talking too much," *The Sun* reported her as saying on October 10. "I damage my voice offstage, not onstage. Onstage I am fine as apparently I am technically great, but when I talk I damage my voice big time. I have got screwed into giving up smoking," Numerous posts from fans begged her to get back on the nicotine gum for the sake of her voice.

Adele's voice problems were such big news that the rumour mill soon went further into overdrive, fuelled by the news that she was too ill to attend the Q Awards ceremony at the end of October to accept the two awards she had scooped: for Best Female and Best Track for 'Rolling In The Deep' (Paul Epworth, the latter song's producer, picked them up on her behalf). Twitter rumours even had it that she was suffering from throat cancer. That particular piece of ghoulish gossip persisted to such an extent that Adele's management was forced to release a statement strenuously denying that the forthcoming surgery she was to undergo was for anything other than a haemorrhaged vocal cord – though not before 'prayforadele' had become a trending topic on Twitter.

Anyone can be struck by voice problems, but singers are naturally particularly vulnerable, and increasingly so given the pressure to tour and perform live in the age of dwindling record sales. Within weeks of Adele cancelling all her remaining 2011 commitments, both country singer Keith Urban and blues star John Mayer announced that they were to undergo similar surgery. The news prompted *The Hollywood Reporter* to pose the question: "Why Are So Many Singers Having Surgery?" and quoted in response Dr. Shawn Nasseri, a Beverly Hills otolaryngologist with a client list including Justin Bieber and Kelly Rowland, as well as a role as the on-call voice doctor for *American Idol* and the US *X Factor*. "Ten years ago, I used to see haemorrhages twice a year; now I see them once a month," he said.

Nasseri put the dramatic rise in voice problems among singers down to the vastly increased demands being made upon them. "When they're successful, there's a lot more of everything – press, promo, they have to tweet, Facebook and chat, they tour and record simultaneously, often late at night... People don't slow down because you've got to strike when the iron is hot. Before, the market would forgive a one- or two-month hiatus; now it's very different."

In seeking treatment for her voice problems, Adele became only the latest in a long line of celebrated singers to do so. While performing in a Broadway run of *Victor/ Victoria* in 1997, Julie Andrews was forced to step down from her leading role after developing nodules on her vocal cords. Subsequent 'routine' surgery to fix the problem damaged their elasticity, limiting her range and her ability to hold notes. Later, in the hope of restoring her singing voice, she came under the care of Steven Zeitels, a pioneering doctor in Boston who was studying ways to restore the loss of elasticity in the vocal cords, which commonly affects singers. Andrews credits Zeitels with giving her back at least some of her singing voice, and has helped him campaign for more research into voice-threatening conditions.

The vocally self-challenging Steven Tyler of Aerosmith – aka 'The Demon of Screamin'' – also underwent pioneering laser surgery under the care of Dr Zeitels to repair a ruptured blood vessel in his throat in 2006. After a few weeks rest, his voice had recovered enough for him to "do the whole Janis Joplin" thing, and for the band to start work on a new album. Tyler's surgery was the subject of a National Geographic Channel documentary entitled *The Incredible Human Machine*.

Roger Daltrey of The Who had severe voice problems at the end of 2009 due to "pre-cancerous dysplasia" on his vocal cords. A month after Zeitels had conducted a laser procedure, and injected some gel-like biomaterial into his vocal cords (and Daltrey had undergone a tough couple of weeks without singing, talking or drinking over Christmas and New Year) the singer was giving it his all on stage with The Who in the half-time show at the 2010 Superbowl.

When it became clear that Adele had a serious problem with her voice, Dr Zeitels – by that time a Harvard professor as well as director of the world-renowned Massachusetts Center for Laryngeal Surgery and Voice Rehabilitation – was the obvious man for the job. In early November, he operated on Adele's vocal cords, later releasing the following statement about her condition. "Adele underwent vocal cord microsurgery to stop recurrent vocal cord haemorrhage from a benign polyp. This condition is typically the result of unstable blood vessels in the vocal cord that can rupture… Dr Zeitels expects Adele to make a full recovery from her laser microsurgery." A couple of weeks later, a mightily relieved Adele blogged: "Thank you for all your positive thoughts and get well wishes. I'm doing really well, on the mend, super happy, relaxed and very positive with it all. The operation was a success and I'm just chilling out now until I get the all clear from my doctors… I best get back to practising my mime show now. Take care, miss you all – Always, Adele xx"

With all her remaining commitments cancelled, 2011 – a year that had started amid such fanfare – ended with a whimper. It was the rise and fall of a big voice. And concern for its owner – still only 23 years old – became something of a national preoccupation, extending well beyond the tabloids and celebrity-fuelled glossies. After all, this was the girl who had been told by a former British prime minister that she was "a light" at the end of the nation's tunnel. Even political weekly *The Spectator* was moved to have its say. In a piece entitled "Get well, Adele", the editor of *The Catholic Herald* no less, dubbed her "the Vera Lynn of the global financial crisis. The throat surgery had better work, because it's going to be difficult to get over the new Depression without her." It was an extraordinary tribute to an ordinary girl from Tottenham who mostly sang pop songs about being disappointed in love, and often pretty miserable ones at that.

In the dark days of early October, Adele had written on her blog: "Singing is literally my life, it's my hobby, my love, my freedom and now my job. I have absolutely no choice but to recuperate properly and fully, or I risk damaging my voice forever… Please have faith in me that this is the only thing I can do to make sure I can always sing and always make music for you to the best of my ability. Truly yours, and yours only forever, Adele xx."

If the price of hearing her voice again was not hearing it for a while, it was a price worth paying.

The 'Big' Issue

People always said about me, "She's not going to get anywhere – she's a fat girl." But it's obviously not an issue. I'm selling records, aren't I?

Adele, 2009

When Adele sounds so good, why is what she looks like even an issue? It's an issue precisely because there are so few young female stars of average proportions in the pop world. As soon as she started attracting attention for her music, the aged 19, sized 14/16 Adele was immediately hailed as some kind of plus-sized role model, whether she wanted to be one or not.

From the very start of her career, Adele has had to accustom herself to probing questions about her size, which would be enough to give most women a complex. Instead she parried them breezily from the beginning. "I'm very confident," she told *The Observer* in January 2008. "Even when I read people saying horrible stuff about my weight... Since I was a teenager, I've been a size 14 or 16, sometimes 18. And it's never been an issue."

Expecting that to put an end to the subject, Adele was taken aback when the questions kept coming. Under the headline 'I Don't Want to Be a Skinny Pop Star', she told the *Daily Mirror* in July: "The focus on my appearance has really surprised me... I make music to be a musician not to be on the cover of *Playboy*."

By the following year, Adele had starting to embrace the focus on her appearance a little more, letting Anna Wintour style her for the Grammys, and taking an interest in designer fashion. Wintour also invited her to be photographed by Annie Leibovitz for the annual 'Shape' issue of US *Vogue*, which celebrates 'Fashion for Every Figure'. Adele talked merrily of her "three bums" in the accompanying interview, but had to defuse a backlash about the Leibovitz photo. Led by Perez Hilton under the headline '*Vogue* Butchers Adele', the magazine stood accused of photoshopping Adele's figure out of all recognition. "Who doesn't get airbrushed?" she countered. "No one says anything when some skinny, blonde, [busty], white-teeth girl gets airbrushed."

Despite this somewhat flippant riposte, Adele had begun to realise how important her own body image was to a certain section of her audience. "Fans are encouraged that I'm not a size zero – that you don't have to look a certain way to do well," she told *Vogue*. It was dawning on Adele that their interest in her size wasn't a sign that they didn't care about her music. It just meant they admired her all the more for being happy in her own skin as well.

As early as summer 2009, Adele had become a fully fledged leading lady of plus-sized fashion. *The Daily Telegraph* ran a special on style "for the fuller figure", citing Adele's "faultless" appearance on stage at the Hollywood Bowl in a form-fitting Barbara Tfank dress as "yet another style triumph for fashion's new generation of plus-size heroines". Adele, the paper said, "is among an emerging group of young female stars who are breaking new ground by demonstrating that 'chic' and 'cutting-edge' are adjectives that now flatter the amply sized rather than just skinny sample-sized fashionistas".

Any fears that her quest to break the US might find Adele in a sneaky quest to boost her image by losing a few pounds were scotched in another interview. "I've been the same [weight] since I was 15 and went on the contraceptive pill. I've got this far without looking like Britney Spears. I think I can go a bit further." According to the interviewer, this last comment was delivered "with a satirical bite worthy of Jay McInerney". A few months earlier, the *Daily Mail* had reported her saying: "You can't go to America and be shit; you could have an amazing figure and they won't buy it. I could wear a bin liner and they'd still like me."

With the weight loss and weight gain of celebrities a perpetual obsession of the gossip magazines, and at a time when eating disorders are on the rise among the young, it's perhaps not surprising that so many have taken to a talented female singer who places so little store by her appearance. Pop music boasts few similar examples. This after all is the high-kitsch, supremely body-conscious era of Katy Perry, Lady

Gaga and Rihanna, where skintight clothes and highly sexualised stage routines are the norm. Against this gaudy and scantily clad backdrop, the resolutely monochrome and properly dressed Adele cuts a striking contrast: a woman who puts on a different kind of show entirely, in which her voice and her lyrics provide all the drama that is needed.

Not that Adele has ever been critical of those female singers who like to let it all hang out. After all, this is a girl who grew up loving the kind of strutting, bubblegum pop of which Katy Perry is just the latest proponent. "The Spice Girls when I was nine were all sexual innuendos. I love it. If you've got it flaunt it, if it works with your music. But I can't imagine having guns and whipped cream coming out of my tits... Even if I had Rihanna's body, I'd still be making the music I make, and that don't go together," she told Q magazine. "I hate that idea, that people might say, 'Look at her – she's only doing well because she's got an amazing body.'"

Adele mostly appears reluctant to be drawn into speaking out explicitly against the pressures young people face to be thin. She continues to prefer to set an example by parrying size questions with bullish disinterest. "I never fell under that spell. I'm size 16, normal... I've got a lot of things on my to-do list and that's right at the bottom. When I can squeeze in time I don't want to go down the fucking gym. I wanna go to the pub with my mates!... It's not even lazy, it's just other things thrill me in life." But on occasion, she has begun – in her inimitable way – to venture just a little more of an opinion. "I wouldn't encourage anyone to be unhealthily overweight just as much as I wouldn't encourage a fucking Ralph Lauren model to suck ice when she feels like fainting... I'm just encouraging people to stop *bullying* each other."

Just as she has come to realise that there are ways to dress and impress with her curvaceous figure, Adele seems of late to have accepted, albeit tacitly, the role-model tag. When *Glamour* magazine put her on the cover of its July 2011 issue, Adele paid tribute to its editor for putting a plus-size girl on the cover. "I think it's pretty brave." *Glamour* was not the only magazine to decide that it was now safe to put Adele there. By the end of the year, she had also graced the covers of *Rolling Stone*, *Q*, *Vogue* and US *Cosmopolitan*.

Vogue once again attracted criticism, however, this time for missing an opportunity to show Adele full-length on the cover, striking though the close-up shot of her head and shoulders was. But in her interview for the same issue, Adele was typically blasé. "I don't have a message. I enjoy being me; I always have done. I've seen people where it rules their lives, you know, who want to be thinner or have bigger boobs, and how it wears them down. And I don't want that in my life. I have insecurities of course, but I don't hang with anyone who points them out to me." It was perhaps the highest-profile, most body-confident statement yet from a woman who had managed to eat pasta *and* appear on the cover of the bible of the fashion industry; a world where size zero had somehow become the rule rather than the exception.

But if Adele had ever hoped that by being blasé about her size the issue would somehow evaporate, she was sadly mistaken. Despite the fact that the *Vogue* interview ranged over a myriad of topics besides her shape, it was those comments of Adele's which the *Daily Mail* chose to highlight under the headline, 'I'm Not Going to Obsess Over Being Thinner'. As *The Guardian* reluctantly conceded, the reality was that the questions were never going to go away. "While it would be nice if the singer didn't feel compelled to defend her weight, often referenced in backhanded journalistic parlance as 'curves', it's also refreshing that she remains candid and unchangeable in her commitment to staying at her natural weight."

The reality is that Adele is damned if she does, and damned if she doesn't. If she answers future questions about her weight with nothing more than a "Next Question", she gives no succour to those fans who now look upon her as an inspiration in their own private battles not to let their lives be ruled by their size. And yet, if she continues to allow it as a significant question when she would so much rather be talking about her music, the risk is that it will remain an issue with which she is forever associated.

The truth is, it probably already is. In November 2011, Lady Gaga was moved to issue a statement via her record label when it emerged that some of her fans had been mocking Adele's size on Twitter, making crude jokes along the lines of: "Confirmed: Gaga will not be wearing her meat dress because she is afraid Adele will eat it." Gaga's response was clear: "Lady Gaga does not approve of bullying anyone for their physical appearance; it goes against everything she stands for."

Compared with Adele, an average-sized woman who makes music that is anything but average, it seems the supremely image-conscious Gaga has it easy.

Chapter 9

The Secret Of Her Success

If my record can make somebody be like, 'Oh, I know exactly what she's talking about,' my job is done.

Adele, 2011

"I want to be making records for ever," Adele had declared back in December 2008. Since that determined early pronouncement, she has grown in stature as a woman of intelligence and beady-eyed focus when it comes to her career. By December 2011, at the end of a phenomenal year, and as if to re-signal her intent, despite her temporary lack of voice, she gazes with supreme curvy confidence from the cover of US *Cosmopolitan*, clad in a low-cut lace and leopard print Dolce & Gabbana number. I ain't going nowhere, she seems to say.

As well as becoming – somewhat despite herself – a powerful role model for averagely proportioned women everywhere, Adele has also been a bombshell for the music industry. Despite the boom in the digital downloading of albums, total album sales have been on the slide for a decade. Given this gloomy context, the storming success of Adele's two records – particularly *21* – is all the more remarkable. As of November 2011, *21* – which could so easily have been that difficult second record

– was by the far the UK's biggest-selling digital album of all time, having sold almost 670,000 copies.

It went out of the gate like a rocket following its release on January 24, achieving two million sales in 12 weeks, to equal the record set by Dido's *Life For Rent*. In July it reached the three million mark, the quickest an album had ever done so, smashing the previous record – held by Oasis' *(What's The Story) Morning Glory* – by a full year. Its combined sales are heading for the four million mark, a figure previously achieved by only a select seven albums in the UK, including such rock-solid classics as *Sgt Pepper's Lonely Hearts Club Band, Dark Side Of The Moon* and *Thriller*. Add to this the phenomenal sales of individual tracks on the album, including over one million for 'Someone Like You', and it's clear that *21* is a record that has found an audience on an unprecedented scale. Any record label currently poised to jump on the bandwagon and "make like Adele" should beware though. As a feature in serious music monthly *The Word* put it: "Her success is so atypical, so counter-intuitive, so beautifully aberrant that any attempts to slipstream her will fall apart because they all lack that crucial elusive ingredient – Adele herself."

But say you did try to bottle it: this prodigious success of hers. What would the magic formula consist of? Those in the business have ventured a few theories. And it's no surprise that talent is the main ingredient. "There's the old cliché that talent, luck, hard work and timing equals success and that's true here," Paul Connolly, president of Universal Music Publishing for UK and Europe, told *Music Week*. "But, to my mind, what makes this album campaign unique is that the talent element of the equation here is so high."

It's hard to argue with that. And thanks to Adele's ballsy persona, and her stated refusals to play festivals or to endorse brands, she appears to be the very antithesis of a modern manufactured pop star, having relied first and foremost on her music to carry her to the top. But while her success is in one sense a "triumph of anti-marketing", Adele's gifts have also been skilfully directed by those around her. So much so that in May 2011, 'Team Adele' – including Richard Russell from XL, Paul Connolly from Universal and Jonathan Dickins from September

Management – was placed top of *The Guardian's* Music Power 100 list of the most important people in British music. (Simon Cowell could only manage third place.) Adele, said the editorial, had only become so powerful "with the help of a team dedicated to making it happen". The 23-year-old Londoner could be seen, it said "as an example of how a brilliant talent – supported by a brilliant team – can still bring millions of people together at the same time, in the simple celebration of great songs." "It is very refreshing to see something so successful done in such a sensitive way," added Cerne Canning, manager of major Scottish indie band Franz Ferdinand and a member of the panel of music industry experts which compiled the list.

Sensitivity notwithstanding, Adele has also been worked hugely hard by her record companies – some would say too hard given what happened to her voice – in terms of public performance and media appearances, particularly in America. In the context of nosediving record sales, making her music connect directly with people was deemed to be vital. In the words of Steve Barnett, chairman of Columbia: "We knew people had to experience her, so we took an old-fashioned approach. She had to go out and play, and because she's so captivating, we felt that if we got the right TV opportunities, she'd be able to cut through."

This is something Rick Rubin had realised too when he told Adele that she needed to capture something of the quality of her live performances when she set about recording *21*. Team Adele has also had several generous slices of luck: Adele's *SNL* performance being seen by 15 million US viewers springs to mind, along with the healthy sales boost given to 'Make You Feel My Love' when it was chosen by several of the contestants on *X-Factor* in 2010. But more importantly – her performances on *Later… With Jools Holland* and at the 2011 Brit Awards being the prime examples – Adele has always delivered momentous performances when it counts most.

XL and Columbia have undoubtedly played their hands well on both sides of the Atlantic. Ultimately though, the reasons for Adele's remarkable feats cannot be ascribed purely to music business insight and acumen. While acknowledging that at heart "it's just music, it's just really good music. There is nothing else. There are no gimmicks, no selling of sexuality," XL founder Richard Russell also believes that Adele's success is going to make people in the music industry "rethink what they should be doing". But, as has already been said, what will be the point if they don't have Adele herself?

In the end, all the best efforts of her record companies would not have achieved half as much if Adele hadn't already been a rare example of an artist able to reach out and captivate people of all ages, all nationalities, and all walks of life with her music. What's more, she does it both in person, and through her recordings. So is it possible to explain just how Adele's music has won so many of us over? It's time to try.

Despite the fact that she's still only in her early twenties, there's something retro about Adele: a timeless quality that provides a salutary tonic in uncertain times. Despite the banter and the garrulousness, and the occasional schoolgirlish bout of gush, she displays maturity, both in her gutsy attitude off stage and her presence upon it, where she has something of the gravitas of an old-fashioned performer.

Perhaps it's in her blood. Growing up, the likeness between Adele and her great-grandmother was often remarked upon – in terms of her looks, her attitude, her "old-fashioned élan". "I never met her but I've been told how she always went with her instinct. Went with her gut. I've always felt connected with her," Adele once said.

In fact Adele has proudly acknowledged herself to be only the latest in a long line of strong women in her family who have survived life's many knock-backs. "All of them have put up with a lot of shit. But they never resented it. They've always been: 'Well, shit happens. Get on with it. Embrace it.'" Everyone loves to celebrate a strong survivor. It's no accident that so many of us know by heart the lyrics of Gloria Gaynor's defiant standard 'I Will Survive', even though it was released 30 years ago. Adele prefers Etta James, but the principle is the same.

Note that there's a difference between embracing adversity and letting it all hang out. In an era when the meltdowns of celebrities – romantic, alcoholic, narcotic – are conducted all too publicly, and often in toe-curling detail, Adele has retained some dignity, even – though it seems a strange word to use for one so upfront – some mystique. Despite increasingly fevered speculation, she has refused to name names when discussing her ex-boyfriends. They were the catalysts for her music, and that's all that matters. What I reveal on stage, she seems to be saying, should be enough for you. The 'who' doesn't matter. It's the 'how': the way in which you deal with falling out of love, and move beyond it, which is important.

Precisely because we don't have 'too much information' about them, Adele's doomed love affairs come across more as the sort of universal heartbreaks that have afflicted almost all of us. By deliberately dampening down gossip of the 'Oh she went out with so and so' variety, and conveying her traumas through her music instead, Adele has succeeded in becoming a kind of 'hurting everywoman' with whom a wide audience is able to identify. Gay or straight, aged 21 or 65, who doesn't, from time to time, need to hear a little cathartic wailing about the "scars of love".

The broadness of Adele's appeal is reflected both in the make-up of the audiences for her live shows, and by the demographic of the much larger numbers who buy her records. After an Adele gig in August 2011, a *Los Angeles Times* reviewer wrote that the crowd consisted of: "women of all shapes and colours. Those wearing stilettos, those wearing sneakers, older Lilith Fair ladies, and girls that take group pics by the restrooms." And "there were more men than expected".

And in a piece for the magazine's October 2011 issue, which featured Adele on the cover, *Vogue* attempted to sum up her universal popularity: "Right now, there is no one who appeals this globally, who connects as much, from the 15-year old boy who's had his heart broken for the first time, to the fifty-something who's on her fourth divorce."

When it comes down to it, the girl from Tottenham's 'life more ordinary', coupled with her voice most extraordinary, is a combination that works on almost anyone. Katy Perry and Rihanna have a certain allure, but it doesn't come from being like the rest of us. Yes, sometimes we want pop music to help us escape from the humdrum, and give us some glitter and Gaga. But in our moments of emotional need, we want it to articulate something of ourselves, and of the everyday hurdles we have to overcome. As website salon.com said of Adele: "The throaty chanteuse doesn't need Gaga's gimmicks. She's got the best weapon of all: she's real."

There's a current school of thought that many record buyers, particularly female ones, are wearying of the raunch and sexualised routines that are now the norm with most girl singers. It's not that they are prudish; it's just that it doesn't represent what it used to. Sisters doing it for themselves are now aplenty in pop music, thanks to the trail blazed by Madonna, but their more extreme antics no longer always appear so empowering for women. When in April 2011 Adele overtook Madonna's record for the longest spell by a female solo artist at the top of the UK album charts, it marked the rise of a different type of sister. Doing it for herself for sure, but rather than choosing to shock us, she had chosen to awe us instead.

What feels empowering now for many women – and for quite a lot of men too – is ordinary-sized Adele's ordinary survival story. She writes and sings beautifully about those common human crises – the ones that happen somewhere every second of the day – in a way that reaches out to the aching, broken hearts of her fans. And soothes them too by saying: I've been there too. And like me, you can get past. "I want people to feel at home when they see me," she said, "to immediately feel comfort."

But somehow, none of it feels cheesy. And perhaps that is because of the yawning contrast between her offstage persona – all gags and garrulousness and great gales of laughter – and the emotionally naked figure she cuts (and "cuts" is often the word) on stage. As Adele herself has recognised, she is the opposite of a stand-up comedian. She displays her inner turmoil for all to see in her songs, and then immediately cracks a joke or tells a filthy anecdote after she's finished singing. But then life itself is composed of such contrasts of emotion.

During a concert in Birmingham in April 2011 – despite having already performed the song countless times – Adele was moved to tears both by her own inner response to 'Make You Feel My Love', and the reaction of her audience. With any other performer, you might be suspicious of the ability to cry so readily on stage, particularly given the quick return to light-hearted banter between songs. But you would never suspect Adele of artifice. Awarding the concert five stars, a reviewer from the *Financial Times* wrote: "The contrast between her down-to-earth personality and the emotional heft of her singing wasn't incongruous. It went to the heart of her appeal. Powerful emotions aren't just the stuff of Greek tragedy: they're part of what it means to be ordinary."

Watch Adele perform 'Someone Like You' and you are transported both into her inner turmoil and hurt when she wrote that song, and into your own inner turmoil and hurt, past or present. Even after she has finished singing, the impact endures, as the piano plays on for a few bars more, and the weight of her words and the power of her voice continue to pull at you. Because you believe her. "The key to great singers is believing every single word they sing," says Jonathan Dickins, one of the first to experience what Adele was capable of. "And I think you believe every word that comes out of her mouth."

It's something that all those who have worked with Adele have found. Paul Epworth who produced 'Rolling In The Deep' says: "It's much easier to try and hide behind a façade or an artistic identity. [Adele] has done something really soulful, and I think it's just connected with people in an age of artifice, and media management, and manufactured pop stars. She's come through as a breath of fresh air."

Sure there is a backlash. Such is the scale of Adele's success that there are plenty of people who say they are sick of her, and the ubiquity of her music. In one national newspaper, she was even held responsible for creating "The New Boring... a ballad-friendly tedial wave destroying everything in its path". Although the tongue-in-cheek commentator then added that, "We must allow The New Boring to take hold, to flourish. It's a good thing, in the long run."

Despite her detractors, Adele's record sales are testament to the fact that millions are lapping her music up. Boundary-pushing and shock tactics are not a priority for all of us, particularly those of us reeling from problems in our own lives, as well as nasty surprises about the state in which our world finds itself. Adele is proof that in such times, a little bit of integrity goes a long way.

In the end, what's required by most of us from our music is genuine talent, from someone real. Adele's ability to make the wonderful music she does, coupled with her resolutely uncultivated image have made her a huge star. She isn't perfect, but that's exactly why there's something about Adele. It's endearing that she swears like a trooper. Smokes like the proverbial chimney. Knocks back red wine – or used to. Admits to picking her nose. Kicks off her shoes as soon as they hurt.

We love it that she went on stage wearing a tampon on her finger. That she once barked with desire at Justin Timberlake. And that she spoils her own dog to bits.

And that, like most of the rest of us, she has been a fool for love.

Reality Chick

The whole idea of being a celebrity: doing my own TV show, launching my own perfume... I suppose I could bottle my piss!

Adele, 2009

If one of the prices of fame is complacency, then Adele hasn't paid it yet. "I always think I can do better. I never love what I do and I don't really rate myself very much," she said in a US radio interview in 2010.

It wasn't the first time she had aired such doubts.

And fame was never her spur. Unlike the wannabe singer or reality show contestant who always declares "I want this so badly", Adele began her career in music with no meaner ambition than perhaps to work in A&R one day, and was persuaded to think of herself as a proper singer only gradually. It wasn't she who posted her early songs on Myspace, and it took persistence on the part of record label XL to convince her that it really was interested in her music before she would agree to a meeting.

Fast forward five and a half years, and global fame is now hers. But Adele remains, she says, "pretty oblivious to it all". Just back from Los Angeles, and a night out at the starry MTV Video Music Awards in September 2011, she went on *The Jonathan Ross Show* and told its host, "I'm not very in touch with the fame side of it. I don't chase none of that, and to be honest it doesn't interest me." The VMAs, she said, had been "a pretty good night out, but I felt pretty out of place and wished I was at home with my girlfriends".

After Adele was signed to XL, and started to make money from her first album, she had a brief flirtation with the celebrity lifestyle, hanging out with the likes of Lily Allen and moving to a posh pad in Notting Hill. Radio 1 DJ Jo Whiley spent time with Adele there, recording a programme for *Live Lounge*. "It was a bijou flat in West London, the kind of area pop stars live when the money comes in. But you could tell her heart wasn't in it – it was too far away from her mum." Within a couple of years, Adele was indeed back living with her mum, in the more familiar surroundings of South London.

Her heart may not have been in Notting Hill, but Adele puts all of it into her electrifying live shows. So much so that she now sells out venues all over Europe and America almost instantly. After two long and highly acclaimed tours for her albums, you might imagine her now to be a relaxed veteran of touring. Far from it. She still doesn't think of herself as a natural performer, and is routinely plagued by crippling stage fright. As her popularity has grown, so has her tendency to shred her nerves.

"I get shitty scared. One show in Amsterdam, I was so nervous I escaped out the fire exit." (In fact, she went missing for about 10 minutes.) "I've thrown up a couple of times. Once in Brussels I projectile-vomited on someone. I've just got to bear it." The vomiting is, she says, a sign of great things to come. "Thing is, the bigger the freakout, the more I enjoy the show."

Matters don't improve once the concert is under way. "My nerves don't really settle until I'm off stage. I mean, the thought of someone spending $20 to come and see me and saying, 'Oh, I prefer the record and she's completely shattered the illusion' really upsets me. It's such a big deal that people come and give me their time."

In backstage footage, shot just before she took the stage for her concert in September 2011 at the 5,000-plus capacity Royal Albert Hall, Adele's tension is almost tangible. Standing in the wings, she looks pale and petrified. After the opening number, 'Hometown Glory', she nevertheless takes to the mike and starts greeting her audience like long lost friends. "Ooh, the Royal Albert fucking Hall!" Despite the vastness of the venue, she wanted, she said, to make her audience feel "like we're just here, having a cup of tea and a takeaway on a Saturday night". Her chatty, take-me-as-you-find-me demeanour on stage – "I don't know what possesses me to chat so much shit" – is a perfected smokescreen, concealing a web of nerves. "I can't help but talk... I try telling my brain: stop sending words to my mouth. But I get nervous and turn into my grandma. Behind the eyes it's pure fear. I find it difficult to believe I'm going to be able to deliver."

Despite the veneer of relaxed informality, Adele finds the whole business of getting up on stage anything but natural. "When I hear artists say, 'Performing is what I'm meant to do,' I think, *What?* This ain't what you're meant to do. It ain't normal." The fact that she has to invest so much emotionally in every performance even to make it on stage in the first place could explain why Adele has such an extraordinary presence. And why, when she sings, you can't help but believe it's all real.

Her stage fright is one reason why Adele has always said she won't play big music festivals, or stadiums, despite the fact that she could now fill them with ease several times over. "I will not do festivals. The thought of an audience that big frightens the life out of me," she told Q magazine. "Say the number 18,000 to her and you can actually see the colour drain out of her face," says Jonathan Dickins. It's not a number he picked out of the air: 18,000 is the capacity of the Hollywood Bowl.

Yet this is one pressure that Adele may now have to bow to, simply because so many people want to see her live. "I get into trouble for not playing bigger venues," she told Jonathan Ross in September 2011. Only a couple of weeks later at London's Hammersmith Apollo, she told the crowd, "This is the last time you'll catch me at a venue like this. These will be my last theatre dates as I'm moving on to arenas." Aside from the boos that her announcement provoked from certain sections of the crowd, performing is not set to get any easier for Adele.

Other aspects of her huge success have proved a challenge for Adele. "I'm in the worst profession – I've got a fear of flying and a fear of cameras," she once quipped. She loathes being followed by photographers. "I hate the paparazzi. I hate them. I think they're disgusting," she told CNN after the Grammys, pretending to spit. Sometimes she can still get out without being recognised, "if I haven't got my lashes and hair up", but she told UK chat-show host Graham Norton in 2011 that she had recently popped into an off-licence and "within two seconds there were like 30 paps outside". She genuinely doesn't understand why she should be hounded. "Look at Meryl Streep, best actress in the world – nobody knows nothing about her, do they?"

On one occasion while living in Notting Hill, Adele was "really pissed off" to be followed home by a phalanx of photographers one night. The next morning they were still outside. Adele went out to give them a piece of her mind, only to discover that they were actually in pursuit of her neighbour, Elle Macpherson.

Adele remains endearingly in awe of other celebrities. Encounters with the likes of Justin Timberlake and Robbie Williams have left her a gibbering wreck. After meeting Beyoncé, she said, "I got down on my knees and cried. I've been listening to her since I was nine, man; it's incredible." The mere sight of Barbara Windsor gave her "butterflies". Standing next to Jay-Z in a queue at the Grammys was "like an actual dream…He smells like money!" But despite her gushing reverence, Adele is also fond of telling stories against herself that puncture the mystique of celebrity: imitating the sound of Jennifer Aniston having a wee in the next door cubicle ("I actually heard her piss come out. And I called her Rachel!"); and blushing about the time she almost ran over P Diddy with a golf cart.

The revered Beyoncé inspired a technique Adele uses to try and ward off her legendary stage fright. When the two singers were about to meet and Adele, completely in awe of the occasion, had "a full-blown anxiety attack", she asked herself what Beyoncé's aggressive and outspoken alter ego Sasha Fierce would do. The moment gave birth to an alter ego of her own: Sasha Carter – a composite of Sasha Fierce and June Carter – whom Adele uses to "pump herself up" before going on stage.

Just as it wouldn't occur to her to consider herself on the same level of celebrity as Beyoncé, Adele also doesn't have any interest in making celebrity demands. When in December 2011, her rider from her US concert tour was leaked to the press, it turned out to be something of a non-story. The most stringent demand therein concerned the drink that should be provided for the crew: "North American beer is *not* acceptable"; a stipulation many Europeans might find perfectly reasonable. Otherwise cereal bars, chewing gum, bottled water and a lighter were about as extravagant as it got.

In the backstage footage from the Royal Albert Hall DVD, Adele shows the cameras round her dressing room. "I'm like an artist who's never sold any records when it comes to my rider. I get some fruit which I don't eat... I don't like fruit, I only like vegetables. I ask for a nice bottle of red wine but I'm not allowed to drink any more so my crew drink that... Water... And honey."

Plenty of celebrities claim they live in the real world of water, honey and cereal bars, but a sense of unreality usually persists around their protestations of normality. When Adele says she likes having a good Hoover round at home, you can easily imagine it to be the case. "I do my own washing. My auntie cleans for me, but I love a good clean as well," she told *Glamour* in July 2011. Adele's efforts to cut through the celebrity crap comes across as genuine. Asked to name her highlight of 2008, Adele said that it was without doubt the fact that *19* had gone to number one in the UK. "My highlights are always stuff in the UK, because then my nan gets to see it."

Although there are unlikely to be any eight-page spreads in *OK Magazine* even for her nan, Adele is terrific value both in press interviews and on TV, being often very funny. But she remains determined not to over-expose herself, particularly now that virtually one in 10 households in the UK owns a copy of *21*. "Quality control is vital. If I did everything, my artistry and music would become diluted... I'd be repeating myself... if I did every TV and every magazine cover I was given the opportunity to do. I only do things I like as well: TV shows I watch and publications I read. I won't do something simply... so I'll sell a few more records."

Adele is similarly determined not to be the face of anything. On her website you can buy a limited selection of merchandise: heart T-shirts; *21* tea towels; 'I'm Tired' Babygros. But there is no Adele perfume (step forward Beyoncé and Katy Perry) and definitely no soft-drinks endorsements à la Duffy and Diet Coke. ("I found it really unnecessary," Adele said of Duffy's promotion, "and it made me see her in another light.") "I don't want to see me plastered everywhere this early in my career... I'm only 23. I might change my mind down the line, but right now, I don't want my name near another brand. If they offered me £10 million, I'd be like, 'Fuck off!' Besides, if I was going to be the face of anything, it should be the face of full-fat Coke!

"There's so many people who believe their own hype and treat people like shit, and if I was ever like that I would absolutely stop doing what I'm doing for a while and go and find myself again. I find it grotesque when people change because of it, but maybe it's because they're not as good at keeping in contact with the people who love them for a reason." When she was asked, at the wise old age of 22, if she had any advice for future holders of the Critics' Choice Award at the Brits, Adele warned against media flimflam. "Don't believe the hype. Don't read any press. Just do it for the reason you started and not because of what everyone's saying."

Now that she is on the verge of playing big arenas, Adele still puts as much store by her connection with her fans as if she was still playing small London pubs. "Although I will never meet most of the people who come to see me live, or buy my records, they're a part of my life. They've changed my life and enable me to do my job."

If Adele has an eye on posterity, it's only so that she'll have something to show off about to her grandchildren. "Sometimes I don't know what possesses me to do it, because albums are like photographs, they're forever. Maybe it's a good thing I'll be able to look back at my records and see how I've grown as a person. And when I'm old and have kids and grandkids and they're going through their angsty teenage stage I was going through at 19, I can be like, 'Listen to that! That's what grandma was doing when she was 19!'"

Success may not have changed Adele, but others in her life haven't always stayed the same. "People start treating you differently," she admitted. Though she says she hates being single, she is all too aware of the dangers of dating now that she is famous and wealthy. "I'm good with my money, and I can spot a bad egg. I've already had... famous people, and people who do normal things, asking if I wanna be with them, and I don't."

A self-declared "emotional wreck" on stage she may be. But off it Adele is a formidable character, who is very sussed about her career. "Right from the beginning she's had a very clear idea of where she wants to be," said Ben Beardsworth, MD of Adele's record label, XL. "It's quite spooky to have that degree of single-mindedness and clarity of vision and confidence and drive." Adele has always remained firmly in the driving seat of her own career." I'll have the final word on everything. I go to the most boring strategy meetings. The more successful you get, the more people work for you. I'd hate for someone to come up and be like, 'Hi, I work with you,' [and for me to say] 'Oh? What do you do?' I like to be really involved in everything... I think I annoy people."

There have been wobbles of course, notably the time Adele cancelled her US tour dates in the summer of 2008 because of what she called her 'Early Life Crisis'. For a time there was a distinct possibility that she might go off the rails, drinking too much and shutting out everything else to be with the man in her life. But after a break and some sober reflection, she got right back on track. Despite the disappointed audiences and impetuousness of her decision, it's hard not to feel sympathy for one who had been thrown the pressures of touring and performing so suddenly, and so young.

"The more successful I get, the more insecurities I'm getting, it's weird... Just about who I am. How I feel about things. I don't know if it's because I'm so blown away that people like what I do, but I just feel like I'm never gonna live up to it." So Adele told *Q* in July 2011. It has all happened so very fast that only now, perhaps, is Adele beginning to realise what she might jeopardise if she doesn't take time out from the spotlight. "I've been doing this since I was 19, and if I do it how I could do it, if I worked my arse off for 10 years, I'd miss my whole twenties. I think that's where my insecurities have been coming in. What if I come out the other end and I dunno who I am?... I don't want to forget to be normal."

And Adele just loves to be normal. Her idea of a perfect day is one spent drinking cider in South London's Brockwell Park with her mates. When Graham Norton suggested in a TV interview in 2011 that Adele was now so famous that she couldn't just take a day off when she felt like it, she was quick to correct him. "Oh no, I've just been on a five-day bender!" At the end of her European tour in the spring of 2011, Adele insisted on flying straight back to Brighton to go to a gig – "with a mate who's a right caner" – despite having a concert in Dublin the following night. When her team protested, she told Q – possibly with her tongue firmly in her cheek – that she had said to them: "I might be in a bit of a state for Dublin… but you work for me, motherfuckers! I need it for my peace of mind."

In December 2011, Adele gave a telling first interview after her vocal cord surgery to mark *Billboard*'s crowning of *21* as the Top Album of 2011, and Adele as its Top Artist. There would be, she said, no new album for two or three years. "I'm just going to lay some concrete, set up home and just 'be' for a bit. I'll disappear and come back with a record when it's good enough."

Adele cannot have remained unaffected by the trauma of losing her voice at such a crucial stage in her career, treating it as another sign perhaps that nothing should be taken for granted. And that to attempt too much too young is unwise. She has already had to grow up fast: with 2011 not just a phenomenal one in terms of music sales, but also a testing one personally. "It's been fucking brilliant and exciting and emotional. Professionally, it's been a year that will define my life forever. But because of the success, obviously things have been unearthed and people have crawled out of the woodwork publicly and privately. But that's to be expected. And those things personally have forced me to address things I probably wouldn't have… until my thirties."

Whatever 2012 brings, Adele remains determined to keep kicking away the high heels of fame in order to stand, as she so often does by the end of concerts, with her stockinged feet firmly on the ground. "When it comes to staying myself -- my career isn't my life, it doesn't come home with me. So it's a piece of piss staying grounded and not being changed by it. The same things I've always liked still satisfy me. My team's the same and my group of friends are the same… I go home and my best friend laughs at me, rather than going to a celebrity-studded party to rub shoulders with people who know me but who I don't know. I'm Z-list when it comes to that shit."

Adele's already vast popularity is only being enhanced by this very ordinariness in the face of her star status. Despite declaring that staying grounded is a "piece of piss", the balancing act between her stellar career and her desire to keep it real will surely remain a delicate one.

"I'm incredibly private but I'm also incredibly honest and I think that creates a kind of 'meet in the middle' respectable ground," she recently declared.

You sense that treading that middle ground won't ever be easy. But if anyone can walk the tightrope, it will be Adele.

Epilogue

When Everyone Cared

Do the work and make the music how you did before anyone cared.
                                                            Adele, 2011

A voice of wonder.

A voice that could stop traffic. A voice that could move mountains. A piercingly poignant singing voice, dripping with soul. A goose-bump inducing voice. A belting voice. An oak-aged voice. A voice that exudes grief. A voice tunefully bruised and resonating with a smoky, Golden Virginia hue.

A thing of aching beauty, adept at flourishes that send chills down your spine, but capable of stripping paint from the walls. A voice like a velveteen cloak. A voice which makes hairs stand on end with its melodious honesty.

A voice so vast, pure and deep-soul powerful it could turn the very tides.

All these things have been written by those who have wrestled their vocabularies to find words capable of describing the stupendous voice that belongs to Adele Laurie Blue Adkins.

At the end of 2011, it had been silent for nearly three months. But there was still plenty of noise about Adele. In late November,

XL released a DVD of Adele's concert at the Royal Albert Hall on September 22. It's true you can hear her battling with her voice to make it go where she wants it to go, and its customary mountain-moving power is often lacking. But it's an electrifying performance nevertheless, and even courageous, given what we now know about the fragile state of her vocal cords.

Though she wasn't able to attend the ceremony which also took place in November, Adele scooped three gongs at the American Music Awards in LA; tying for the top haul of the night along with Taylor Swift. And on December 1, the advent of a remarkable, but not entirely unexpected, six Grammy nominations: Album of the Year and Best Pop Vocal Album for *21*; Song of the Year, Record of the Year and Best Short Form Music Video for 'Rolling In The Deep'; and Best Pop Solo Performance for 'Someone Like You'. Only one female artist has ever won six Grammys in one year, and the name of that artist is Beyoncé. A woman of whom Adele is, it seems, still endearingly in awe.

In 2012, Adele will be back. Her fans hope, and trust, that her voice will be as wondrous as ever. And if she feels any pressure to deliver in future, so far Adele hasn't shown it. "I don't really care about expectations... I'm not expecting my next record to be as big as this one." In the light, perhaps, of what she has learned from her collaborations on *21*, her own creative input will, she has said, be paramount. "I want it to be quite acoustic and piano-led. I want to write it, record it all, produce it all and master it on my own."

Why does she think this is her time? Adele was asked during an interview for the landmark 300th issue of Q for which she also appeared on the cover, photographed by Rankin in a deep purple gown.

"Maybe people know I just like music... I think I remind people of themselves," she said.

I think she does too. Apart, of course, from that voice of wonder.

Acknowledgements

My thanks to everyone at Omnibus Press; Mathew Lyons for judicious and patient editing; my agent Sarah Such for being ever wise and encouraging; Jon Scott for musical notes; Sarah Scott for coffees and chinwags; Nikki Michael for technical support; Anne Joseph & Jane Bailey for writerly support and good counsel; Christina Stead for being 'My Same'; Kane's Records in Stroud for being a great indie record shop; David, Alexander & Julia Brookes for life, and soul, and being loyal fans.

Source Notes

Source Notes
All interviews are with Adele, unless otherwise stated. Unsourced quotes from Adele are taken from interviews on her website, www.adele.tv, or from her *Live At The Royal Albert Hall* DVD

Prologue
"I desperately want more gravitas," David Joseph, *The Guardian*, November 8, 2010
"most life-changing night of my life," interview by Chris Moyles, BBC Radio 1, July 5, 2011

One: Dreams
"arty", *Daily Telegraph,* April 27, 2008
"she fell pregnant", *The Observer,* March 27, 2011
"a really big Welsh guy", *The Observer,* January 27, 2008
"I had, like, 30 cousins…", *Daily Telegraph,* April 27, 2008
"Embarrassingly, my mum…", *The Sun,* January 18, 2008
"Even though some people think they're uncool…", *Now* magazine, March 2, 2011
"They're the reason I wanted to be an entertainer…", YouTube, http://www.youtube.com/watch?NR=1&v=iaDA5uvtwN8

"The people seemed really pretentious...", *The Times*, December 28, 2007

"They were like, bloody hell, you're a *singer.*"*Q,* May 2008

"I had never heard...", www.spinner.com/2010/12/23/adele-defining-moments/

"Although Pink will stop at absolutely nothing...", review, *NME*, http://www.nme.com/reviews/artistKeyname/6854

"I was trying to be cool...", *The Sun*, January 18, 2008

"Initially... I loved the way she looked...", *Blues & Soul*, http://www.bluesandsoul.com/feature/302/the_futures_looking_rosie_for_adele

"took over my mind and body", *Rolling Stone*, April 28, 2011

"Chart music was all I ever knew...", *Daily Telegraph,* April 27, 2008

"amazing Faith Evans-type singer", *Blues & Soul*, July 2008

"They didn't really encourage me...", *The Times*, December 28, 2007

"I wanted to go to Sylvia Young....", Q, May 2008.

"a school full of kids...", *The Guardian*, January 27, 2008

"That Leona Lewis...", *The Sun*, January 18, 2008

"Some of the people there are atrocious, really bad," *The Times*, December 28, 2007

"Nobody at the BRIT School taught me how to sing", Q, May 2008

"I'd turn up to school four hours later..." *Rolling Stone*, April 28, 2011

"doing pirouettes in the fucking hallway", *Vogue,* October 2011

"Most artists haven't got a clue...", *The Times*, December 28, 2007

"I heard her playing this shrieky saxophone," Shingai Shoniwa, *Daily Mail*, 22 August 2011

"We lived right next door to each other...", ibid

Two: Bluebirds Fly Out

"I wanted to help other people sell records," *Rolling Stone*, January 22, 2009

"some internet perv", *Vogue*, October 2011

"That was when we got fucking excited", *The Observer, March 27,* 2011

"stomach cramps the day after", ibid

"I listened and threw in some ideas...", Jonathan Dickins, *Vogue,* October 2011

"We met in a very unglitzy, unshowy world…", Jack Peñate, http://news.bbc.co.uk/newsbeat/hi/music/newsid_8045000/8045397.stm

"I owe so much to Jack…", *The Sun*, January 18, 2008

"I was overwhelmed by the deal…", *Billboard*, http://www.billboard.com/news/chasing-adele-1003816595.story#/news/chasing-adele-1003816595.story

"I went to the pub…", *Rolling Stone*, January 22 2009

"When we fall for somebody…" Alison Howe, *The Guardian*, November 23, 2007 http://www.guardian.co.uk/music/2007/nov/23/popandrock1

"When my mum came backstage…", *The Times*, December 28, 2007

"They usually put you in the middle…", *The Guardian*, November 23, 2007

"when she opens her gob…", review, Drowned In Sound, drownedinsound.com/directory/artists/Adele

"The expectations around this single…", Jonathan Dickins, *Music Week*, http://www.musicweek.com/story.asp?storycode=1031776

"It wasn't stellar performances…", review, *The Independent*, February 5, 2008

"I was obsessed with him", Radio 1 Newsbeat, November 12, 2008

"the first artist we've ever had playlisted on Radio 2", Richard Russell, *The Times*, December 28, 2007

"really weird…", ibid

"It's frightening how in control he is…", *Time Out*, January 22, 2008

"The first thing that ensnares listeners…", review, BBC, http://news.bbc.co.uk/1/hi/entertainment/7168252.stm

"identikit bands…", Paul Rees, BBC, http://news.bbc.co.uk/1/hi/entertainment/7169307.stm

"I can't believe I did a peace sign on TV…", *The Observer*, January 22, 2008

"Nah, I'm an opportunist…", YouTube, http://www.youtube.com/watch?v=PCIV9u0EcWk

"Outstanding debut…", review, *The Observer*, January 20, 2008

"less like a launch…", review, *The Guardian*, January 25, 2008

"passably decent debut…", review, *The Independent*, January 25, 2008 "precious little on the album…", *NME*, http://www.nme.com/reviews/adele/9433

"a genuinely touching, maturely considered…", review, BBC, http://www.bbc.co.uk/music/reviews/6pf9

"I read them at the beginning…", *Time Out*, January 22, 2008

"I keep getting called…", *Metro*, http://www.metro.co.uk/showbiz/85604-adele-not-bothered-by-amy-comparison

"I've been tipped by the industry…", *Time Out*, January 22, 2008

"I never made any claims about my success," *Q*, May 2008

"The breath-taking assurance…", *The Sunday Telegraph*, February 3, 2008

"Adkins has had the kind of attention…", review, *The Guardian*, January 31, 2008

"I'm not going to burn myself out…", *Q*, May 2008

"'Valerie'…", YouTube, http://www.youtube.com/watch?v=TZFhst2AHGA&feature=fvst

"It's so nice to be here…", *NME*, February 20, 2008

"Fucking idiots…", *Q*, May 2008

19: About A Boy

"It's like a child's view on love", *The Independent*, February 5, 2008

"oak-aged voice and Botticelli face", *NME*, February 1, 2008

"The best ones for me are 'Debut' by Björk", *Blues & Soul*, July 2008

"To me this album does very much represent my age", ibid

"Even when I was little…", *Daily Telegraph*, January 31, 2008

"I hate – I'm actually offended by…", *Blues & Soul*, July 2008

"It took a lot from me…", http://blogcritics.org/music/article/interview-adele-singer-and-songwriter/page-2/#ixzz1Z9T2IW3khe

"I will sit in my room…", *The Guardian*, January 27, 2008

"The idea with XL…", Richard Russell, *The Guardian*, November 23, 2007

"I never at any stage thought…", *Blues & Soul*, July 2008

Jim Abbiss interview, *Sound on Sound*, September 2006

"It's about: should I give up…", *The Sun*, January 18, 2008

"because I wanted that radio song…", *Blues & Soul*, July 2008

"I went to Eg's studio the next morning…", ibid

"some weirdo on the Net", *Daily Mail*, September 10, 2008

"a booming shout-out...", *NME*, February 1, 2008

"starts out sounding almost like vintage Portishead...", *The Observer*, January 20, 2008

"I thought I'd be best known for more acoustic songs...", *Blues & Soul*, July 2008

"Sacha gave me my education...", James Blunt, www.sachaskarbek.com

"When I first played the song...", *Blues & Soul*, July 2008

"She said, I've got this song...", Mark Ronson, Q, May 2008

'When Mark Ronson jolts Adele...", review, Digital Spy, http://www.digitalspy.co.uk/music/albumreviews/a88205/adele-19.html

"With its flickering, panoramic production...", review, *NME*, February 1, 2008

"you feel like bringing her a saucer of HobNobs...", review, *The Independent*, February 5, 2008

"No one has put words and music...", review, *The Times*, January 25, 2008

"show-stopping vocal", review, Digital Spy, http://www.digitalspy.co.uk/music/albumreviews/a88205/adele-19.html

"a textbook done-me-wrong Motown pastiche", review, *NME*, February 1, 2008

"a spare ballad undermined by greeting-card lyrics...", review, *Rolling Stone*, May 22, 2001

"summons a passion...", review, *The Observer*, January 20, 2008

"I don't even remember the reason...", *Live At The Royal Albert Hall DVD*, 2011

"A combination of that voice...", Jonathan Dickins, Hit Quarters, www.hitquarters.com/index.php3?page=intrview/opar/intrview_Jonathan_Dickins_Interview.html#ixzz1af3diod0

"It was kind of about me and my mum...", *Blues & Soul*, July 2008

"I was really pissed...", Q, May 2008

"It's about London...", *The Sun*, January 18, 2008

"That piano, still, pokes at the heart...", review, Drowned In Sound, http://drownedinsound.com/releases/12483/reviews/2874741-adele-19

"killer piano riff…", review, *NME*, February 1, 2008

"The way she stretched the vowels…", review, *The Observer*, January 20, 2008

"already *19* sounds like the work…", Q, May 2008

"He loves it…", *The Sun*, January 18, 2008

Three: Chasing Sidewalks

"Yesterday we were outside…", *Nylon,* July 2009

"The instant success…", *The Independent*, February 5, 2008

"I'm learning about the US all the time…", Jonathan Dickins, Hit Quarters, http://www.hitquarters.com/index.php3?page=intrview/opar/intrview_Jonathan_Dickins_Interview.html#ixzz1ZiTvnvbh

"I love singing…", *NOW*, March 27, 2008

"I just can't stop thinking about how amazing her voice is…", review, http://www.musicsnobbery.com/2008/03/adele-joes-pub.html

"I have just seen a star in the making", review, *Goldmine*, http://www.goldminemag.com/tag/joes-pub

"Thanks so much for coming…", review, *The Independent*, May 7, 2008

"During her hour-long set…", review, *Rolling Stone*, June 13, 2008

'I want to write my second album in New York…", *The Daily Mirror*, July 20, 2008

"Everything is happening so fast…", blogcritics, http://blogcritics.org/music/article/interview-adele-singer-and-songwriter/page-2/#ixzz1ZigYKwju

"Chasing Pavements is a very English phrase…", *Blues & Soul*, July 2008

"Four hours later I emerged…, Oh my, I was flying down Broadway, very drunk", *Daily Telegraph*, December 10, 2008

"This buzzed-about British bird…", review, *Entertainment Weekly*, June 6, 2008

"six stinky guys…", *Daily Telegraph*, December 10, 2008

"I did the Radio 1 Live Lounge…", *The Daily Mirror*, July 20, 2008

"It was the biggest deal in my entire life…", Digital Spy, http://www.digitalspy.co.uk/music/news/a305347/adele-writing-album-broke-my-heart.html

"It was one of the best shows ever…", Battery In Your Leg,

http://batteryinyourleg.com/blog/2008/11/18/adele/

"I got in trouble for wasting people's time...", *Daily Mail*, February 13, 2009

"It had got to the stage...", *Daily Mail*, February 13, 2009

"We refer to that period...", *Nylon*, July 2009

"I was really unhappy at home...", contactmusic, http://www.contactmusic.com/news/adele-explains-2008-booze-love-meltdown_1105845

"my whole mouth goes red...", *The Observer*, January 27, 2008

"I try not to moan about it...", *Observer Music Monthly*, March 15, 2009

"The album... arrived in June...", *Richmond Times-Dispatch*, October 23, 2008

"Some Secret Service person...", *Nylon*, July 2009

"For two months now...", *Entertainment Weekly*, Ocotber 20, 2008

"I thought, 'Wow...", Jonathan Dickins, Radio 4

"Adele's combination of sultry vocals...", *Richmond Times-Dispatch*, October 23, 2008

"not really my era...", *Richmond Times-Dispatch*, October 23, 2008

"I loved him from the minute I met him", *Herald Sun*, January 13, 2011

Four: And The Award Goes To

"I miss Utterly Butterly...", *The Guardian*, March 15, 2009

"Even though I'm given time to be on my own...:, contactmusic, http://www.contactmusic.com/news/adele-admits-to-struggling-with-second-album_1086551

"He was really stingy...", US *Vogue*, April 2009

"It would be lovely to get one..." BBC, http://news.bbc.co.uk/1/hi/entertainment/7767508.stm

"What I meant is that a Grammy is like an Oscar..." *Los Angeles Times*, December 9, 2008

"The cup of tea ...", *The Independent*, December 23, 2008

"with such sincerity...", review, melophobe, http://www.melophobe.com/concert-reviews/adele-somerville-theatre-somerville-ma/

"Convincing in making one believe...", review, *Variety*, February 1, 2009

"I'm ready to go home now...", *Observer Music Monthly*, March 15, 2009

"It's a baritone ballad…", *Sunday Times*, January 9, 2011

"I just like pooed myself…", CBC Arts Online, www.youtube.com/watch?v=aHBdTfEkICk

"I had to go on stage…", Starpulse, January 13, 2011 http://www.starpulse.com/news/index.php/2011/01/13/singer_adele_still_embarrassed_by_tamp

"like a blonde blur…", *The Guardian*, March 15, 2009

"Everyone was like…", Radio 1 Live Lounge

"When she performs…", Hamish Bowles, US *Vogue*, April 2009

"out of body experience…", *Daily Mail*, January 20, 2011

"I called her afterwards…", *Glamour*

"I'm going to go and put my jeans on…", YouTube, http://www.youtube.com/watch?v=pOP3wk9tH98

"by far my favourite record…", YouTube, http://www.youtube.com/watch?v=GPCvBuE-36o

"It just blew me away…", *Nylon*, July 2009

"Maybe I should get two milkshakes…", US *Vogue*, April 2009

"With the troubles…", *Nylon*, July 2009

"Last time I was at the Brit award…", BBC, http://news.bbc.co.uk/newsbeat/hi/music/newsid_7884000/7884130.stm

"The year is only three months old…", DFW, http://www.dfw.com/2009/03/16/107549/review-adele-is-flawless-in-dallas.html

"On these long, long bus journeys…", MSN, http://music.uk.msn.com/xclusives/adele/article.aspx?cp-documentid=155829034

"I love her so much…", CBC Arts Online, www.youtube.com/watch?v=aHBdTfEkICk

"I believe every single word…," ibid

"an alien from outer space", review, *Los Angeles Times*, June 29, 2009

Handbags And Gladrags

"I've never looked at a magazine cover…", *the gentlewoman*, Spring/Summer 2011

"Five hundred quid, I think it was…", US *Vogue*, April 2009

"I'm worried I'm going to get drunk…", *Daily Mail*, September 10, 2008

"The striped dress…", review, *Entertainment Weekly*, September 20, 2008, http://popwatch.ew.com/2008/10/20/adele-snl-sales/.

"Adele is the antithesis…", *The Daily Mirror*, July 20, 2008

"I was like, 'I've got five bums…'", *Los Angeles Times*, June 21, 2009

"Who doesn't get airbrushed?", ibid

"I met her when she was just 20…", Barbara Tfank, *Vogue*, October 2011

"She had this very cool beehive…", Barbara Tfank, E-Online, February 9, 2009, http://uk.eonline.com/news/marc_malkin/adeles_grammy_weekend_from_band-aids/99159#ixzz1drojihHD

"She is more like Marilyn Monroe…", Barbara Tfank, *Daily Mail*, February 13, 2009

"'Something by Michael Kors…'", *Daily Mail*, February 13, 2009

"I like looking nice…'", ibid

"I thought I'd be the last person…", YouTube, http://www.youtube.com/watch?v=MkbbTrBX3Ck

"Before, I was like, what's the point…", Hollywood Worx, June 21, 2009, http://hollywoodworx.com/archives/1176

"rattle off the names of her favourite labels…" *Nylon*, July 2009

"much rather dress comfortable…", Hollywood Worx, June 21, 2009, http://hollywoodworx.com/archives/1176

"most inspiring names to dress…", Barbara Tfank, *Vogue*, October 2011

"The first time I met Adele…", Gaelle Paul quoted in *Los Angeles Times*, June 21, 2009, http://articles.latimes.com/2009/jun/21/image/ig-adele21/2

"If they give me free stuff…", ibid

"I just thought, oh fuck it…", YouTube, http://www.youtube.com/watch?v=Do5vPsALD-g&feature=relmfu

"The matey chat…", review, *The Observer*, July 10, 2011

"I don't play the guitar any more…", review, New Reviews, http://www.new-reviews.co.uk/?p=4851.

"I feel like a woman…", Q, July 2011

"Song-bird Adele…," *Heat*, December 10, 2010, http://www.heatworld.com/Star-Style/2010/12/the-royal-variety-performance---what-they-wore/?iid=6

"Not only did Adele tear down the VMAs…", *Rolling Stone*, www.rollingstone.com/music/photos/the-2011-mtv-video-music-awards-best-and-worst-dressed-20110829/best-dressed-adele-0563099#ixzz1frDRx0l4

"Adele wore the exact same black shift dress…", *Examiner*, http://www.examiner.com/music-industry-in-los-angeles/2011-mtv-vmas-10-worst-dressed-include-justin-bieber-lady-gaga-adele-photos#ixzz1frFIFpQD

"My life is full of drama…", *Rolling Stone*, April 201

Five: Dog Days

"But of course, it ended…", *Nylon*, February 2011

"They know I won't deliver…", Smooth Radio backstage interview, January 12, 11 http://www.youtube.com/watch?v=IIDT7skbtt0

"I moved out and tried to be all cool…", Digital Spy, http://www.digitalspy.co.uk/showbiz/news/a181237/adele-moves-back-in-with-her-mother.html

"I got loads of cookery books…", YouTube, http://www.youtube.com/watch?NR=1&v=WiMH445103E

"He gets scared…", Digital Spy, http://www.digitalspy.co.uk/showbiz/news/a181237/adele-moves-back-in-with-her-mother.html

"He made me an adult…" *Rolling Stone*, April 24, 2011

"He did it after he heard…", review, CanCulture, http://www.canculture.com/2011/05/19/adele-plays-first-arena-gig-at-acc/

"Well this ain't going to work…", 89.3 The Current, Minnesota Public Radio, October 21, 2010, http://minnesota.publicradio.org/display/web/2010/10/21/adele-live/

"I never get angry…", *Calgary Sun*, March 13, 2011, http://www.calgarysun.com/entertainment/music/2011/03/10/17569906.html

"She was obviously quite fragile…", Paul Epworth, *Rolling Stone*, November 28, 2011

"as pathetic as the first…", CBC Arts Online, www.youtube.com/watch?v=aHBdTfEkICk

"All my friends…," *Rolling Stone*, April 24, 2011

"Boys. I've still got the same problems…", Digital Spy, http://www.digitalspy.co.uk/music/news/a158208/adele-halfway-through-new-album.html http://www.youtube.com/watch?v=aHBdTfEkICk

"I've got a big cabinet…", *Elle*, June 15, 2009

"I was like, 'Right…'", *Variety*, February 5, 2011, http://www.variety.com/article/VR1118031551

"I made a huge effort…", MSN, January 12, 2011, http://music.uk.msn.com/xclusives/adele/article.aspx?cp-documentid=155829693

"When I was doing *19*…", *Variety*, February 5, 2011, http://www.variety.com/article/VR1118031551

"This time, nobody did anything wrong…", *Daily Mail*, January 20, 2011

Six: California Blue

"It's been an exciting experience…", Paul Epworth, BBC6 Music, February 15, 2010

"most infamous producers of modern music", www.discogs.com http://www.discogs.com/artist/Rick+Rubin

"medium-size bear with a long, grey beard", *The New York Times*, September 2, 2007

"defined my youth", *Daily Mail*, January 20, 2011

"He is overrated…", Matt Bellamy, blabbermouth.net, November 22, 2011, http://www.roadrunnerrecords.com/blabbermouth.net/news.aspx?mode=Article&newsitemID=166451

"Shall we do a record together?…", www.clashmusic.com, January 17, 2011, http://www.clashmusic.com/news/adele-on-rick-rubin-team-up

"I felt like going…", jam.canoe.ca, http://jam.canoe.ca/Music/Artists/A/adele/2011/03/10/17569861.html

"I think it was a challenge for both of us…", www.spin.com, May 28, 2010, http://www.spin.com/articles/exclusive-adele-studio

"I'm too pale for the sun…", *Calgary Sun*, March 13, 2011 http://www.calgarysun.com/entertainment/music/2011/03/10/17569906.html

"It was a very surreal experience…", *The Sun*, October 15, 2011

"When he's speaking…", www.spin.com, May 28, 2010

"He was just so wise…", www.clashmusic.com, January 17, 2011, http://www.clashmusic.com/feature/hometown-hero-adele-interview

"Everything I do…", Rick Rubin, *The New York Times,* September 2, 2007

"Her voice is a direct conduit…", Zane Lowe, *The Guardian,* November 23, 2007

"You can feel her life force…", Rick Rubin, *Billboard,* January 28, 2011, http://www.billboard.com/#/features/adele-the-billboard-cover-story-1005015182.story?page=2

"It's all about the song…", www.spin.com, May 28, 2010, http://www.spin.com/articles/exclusive-adele-studio

"There was no 'listen-up' referencing…", MSN Music, January 12, 2011, http://music.uk.msn.com/xclusives/adele/article.aspx?cp-documentid=155829693

"But when we covered it…", *Variety,* February 5, 2011, http://www.variety.com/article/VR1118031551

"It's very raw…", ibid

"Then I played it for her…", ibid

"I didn't want to be travelling loads…", www.clashmusic.com, January 17, 2011, http://www.clashmusic.com/feature/hometown-hero-adele-interview

"I was, like, 'Who the fuck does he think he is?'…", *The Hollywood Reporter,* August 18, 2011, http://www.hollywoodreporter.com/review/adele-at-palladium-concert-review-225095

"*19,* that album was so absolutely mind-blowing…", Ryan Tedder, *BBC Radio 1 Newsbeat,* December 14, 2009, http://www.bbc.co.uk/newsbeat/10003361

"…through the Ryan Tedder machine…", ibid

"…just clicked…", Jonathan Dickins *Music Week,* May 28, 2011, http://www.musicweek.com/story.asp?sectioncode=2&storycode=1045395

"Louie, her really sweet dog…", Fraser T Smith, *BBC Radio 1 Newsbeat,* June 10, 2011, http://www.bbc.co.uk/newsbeat/13717976

"Adele truly is the most talented person…", Greg Wells, www.americansongwriter.com, November 21, 2011, http://www.americansongwriter.com/2011/11/adele-one-and-only/

"She is a very visionary artist…", Dan Wilson, www.spinner.com, March 24, 2011, http://www.spinner.com/2011/03/24/dan-wilson-adele/

"He said something very true about her…", Dan Wilson, Cities97, August 23, 2011

"I've listened to *21* a lot…", ibid

"I was exhausted from being such a bitch…", MTV, February 18, 2011, http://www.mtv.com/news/articles/1658345/adele-21.jhtml

"I didn't keep up my lessons…", *Metro*, February 23, 2011, http://www.metro.co.uk/showbiz/856432-adele-bitter-break-up-drove-me-to-drink#ixzz1f1MDBXlW

"Well, I would still be singing in the shower…", www.out.com, http://www2.out.com/features/2011/05/Adele-Lady-Sings-The-Blues/?slideshow_title=Adele-Lady-Sings-The-Blues&theID=1#Top

21: About A Woman

"I was really angry…", interview with www.people.com as quoted in *Metro*, February 23, 2011, http://www.metro.co.uk/showbiz/856432-adele-bitter-break-up-drove-me-to-drink#ixzz1eMZjKNqv

"My record is about 80% me on my own…", Smooth Radio, January 12, 2011, http://www.youtube.com/watch?v=IIDT7skbtt0

"I'm quite throwaway of my own material…", *Rolling Stone*, February 17, 2011, http://www.rollingstone.com/culture/blogs/rolling-stone-video-blog/adele-on-21-the-songs-on-here-are-the-most-articulate-ive-ever-written-20110217#ixzz1gGCZEEAt

"People always think I'm a serious person…", MSN Music, January 12, 2011, http://music.uk.msn.com/xclusives/adele/article.aspx?cp-documentid=155829034

"I feel a lot bolder now…", Smooth Radio, January 12, 2011, http://www.youtube.com/watch?v=IIDT7skbtt0

"I'm more interested in having a body of work…", BBC6 Music, October 7, 2009, http://www.bbc.co.uk/6music/news/20091007_adele.shtml

"I haven't made a country record…", BBC Radio 1 Live Lounge, January 27, 2011, http://www.bbc.co.uk/programmes/p00dkmnv

"Contemporary records can take three minutes…", *Daily Telegraph*, January 19, 2011

"She'd definitely been exposed to things…", Paul Epworth, *Billboard*, January 28, 2011, http://www.billboard.com/#/features/adele-the-billboard-cover-story-1005015182.story?page=1

"I really got into how gritty and dirty she was…", 89.3 The Current, Minnesota Public Radio, October 21, 2010, http://minnesota.publicradio.org/display/web/2010/10/21/adele-live/

"This time, nobody did anything wrong…", *Daily Mail*, January 20, 2011, http://www.dailymail.co.uk/tvshowbiz/article-1349112/Im-failure--thats-I-sing-Never-mind-hits-Adele-reveals-fuelled-pain-insecurity.html#ixzz1eQzhGidM

"The experience of writing this record was quite exhausting…", *Daily Telegraph*, January 19, 2011

"I finally was at home…", www.clashmusic.com, January 17, 2011, http://www.clashmusic.com/feature/hometown-hero-adele-interview

"I'm a control freak…", *Daily Mail*, January 20, 2011

"It was old school…", ibid

"It was an… obvious title…", idolator.com, November 23, 2010, http://idolator.com/5694122/adele-idolator-interview-21

"I do love it…", MSN Music, January 12, 2011, http://music.uk.msn.com/xclusives/adele/article.aspx?cp-documentid=155829034

"And I think some of the songs on here…", *Rolling* Stone, February 17, 2011, http://www.rollingstone.com/culture/blogs/rolling-stone-video-blog/adele-on-21-the-songs-on-here-are-the-most-articulate-ive-ever-written-20110217#ixzz1gGCZEEAt

"I kept going, 'Feel my heartbeat, Paul!'…", jam.canoe.ca, http://jam.canoe.ca/Music/Artists/A/adele/2011/03/10/17569861.html

"and be like, 'Shit, it sounds like she is going to kill him…'" *the gentlewoman*, Spring and Summer 2011

"I'm really sarcastic, really cheeky…", MSN Music, January 12, 2011, http://music.uk.msn.com/xclusives/adele/article.aspx?cp-documentid=155829034

"When I go and see a live show…", 89.3 The Current, Minnesota Public Radio, October 21, 2010, http://minnesota.publicradio.org/display/web/2010/10/21/adele-live/

"She hooted, she hollered…", review, *The Observer*, January 23 2011

"…a bit of a mouthful…", www.blackbookmag.com, January 31, 2011, http://www.blackbookmag.com/music/adele-opens-up-about-the-relationship-that-inspired-her-new-album-1.37349

"That's how I felt, you know…", *Rolling Stone*, February 17, 2011 http://www.rollingstone.com/culture/blogs/rolling-stone-video-blog/adele-on-21-the-songs-on-here-are-the-most-articulate-ive-ever-written-20110217

"A lot has happened to her since her first record…", Rick Krim, *Billboard,* January 28, 2011, http://www.billboard.com/features/adele-the-billboard-cover-story-1005015182.story#/features/adele-the-billboard-cover-story-1005015182.story

"It's about this boy I met in the summer…", CBC Arts Online, May 1, 2009, http://www.youtube.com/watch?v=aHBdTfEkICk

"Motown on steroids…", review, about.com, http://top40.about.com/od/adele/fr/Adele-21.htm

"…a swamp song so perfectly shadowy…", review, *NME*, January 24, 2011

"As much as I love *19*…", Ryan Tedder, *Billboard,* January 28, 2011 http://www.billboard.com/features/adele-the-billboard-cover-story-1005015182.story#/features/adele-the-billboard-cover-story-1005015182.story

"…not to be taken seriously…", idolator.com, November 23, 2010, http://idolator.com/5694122/adele-idolator-interview-21

"'Turning Tables' sets Adele in a class of her own…", review, www.thecouchsessions.com, February 18, 2011, http://www.thecouchsessions.com/2011/02/album-review-adele-21/

"This is a ballad that will try its hardest…", review, www.contactmusic.com, http://www.contactmusic.com/album-review/adele-21

"When I was in the studio in Malibu…", www.cmt.com, February 4, 2011, http://www.cmt.com/news/country-music/1657301/adele-inspired-by-lady-antebellums-need-you-now.jhtml

"With its mellow verses…", www.mtv.co.uk, January 21, 2011, http://www.mtv.co.uk/news/adele/254508-adele-21-track-by-track-review

"By giving in to a fickle heart…", review, eyeweekly.com, February 16, 2011, http://archives.eyeweekly.com/ondisc/article/110872

"…elements of Phil Spector in his heyday…", review, noripcord.com, January 25, 2011, http://www.noripcord.com/reviews/music/adele/21

"…the only real misfire on the album…", review, musicom.com, http://www.musicomh.com/albums/adele-2_0111.htm

"…a powerful, forward-looking catharsis…", review, about.com, http://top40.about.com/od/adele/fr/Adele-21.htm

"Aretha Franklin vibe…", review, www.soulculture.co.uk, January 26, 2011, http://www.soulculture.co.uk/reviews/adele-21-album-review/

"Rolling Stones-esque bar-room gospel", MSN Music, January 12, 2011, http://music.uk.msn.com/xclusives/adele/article.aspx?cp-

"…tempt you to call your last love…", review, www.thecouchsessions.com, February 18, 2011, http://www.thecouchsessions.com/2011/02/album-review-adele-21/

"To have her singing her ideas the way she sounds…", Greg Wells, www.americansongwriter.com, November 21, 2011, http://www.americansongwriter.com/2011/11/adele-one-and-only/

"'One and Only' might be your wedding anthem…", review, www.thecouchsessions.com, February 18, 2011 http://www.thecouchsessions.com/2011/02/album-review-adele-21/

"It was really weird because…", www.popservations.com, February 27, 2011, http://www.popservations.com/cover-story/adele-covers-the-cure/

"She'd disown me if she didn't like it…", *Variety*, February 5, 2011, http://www.variety.com/article/VR1118031551

"I think it's really important…", *Rolling Stone*, February 17, 2011, www.rollingstone.com/culture/blogs/rolling-stone-video-blog/adele-on-21-the-songs-on-here-are-the-most-articulate-ive-ever-written-20110217#ixzz1ftOfybnB

"We were so intense I thought we would get married…", Q, July 2011

"We didn't try to make it open-ended…", Dan Wilson, *Billboard*, January 28, 2011, http://www.billboard.com/features/adele-the-billboard-cover-story-1005015182.story#/features/adele-the-billboard-cover-story-1005015182.story?page=2

"It's a place with a high ceiling…", Dan Wilson, www.startribune.com, Sepetember 8, 2011, http://www.startribune.com/entertainment/blogs/129508563.html

"By the end of the second day…", Dan Wilson, Cities97, August 23, 2011

"When she sings…", ibid

"After I wrote it, I felt more at peace…", Q, July 2011

"It may be a cliché…", review, MTV, January 21, 2011, http://www.mtv.co.uk/news/adele/254508-adele-21-track-by-track-review

"It's my favourite song that I've ever written…", www.blackbookmag.com, January 31, 2011, http://www.blackbookmag.com/music/adele-opens-up-about-the-relationship-that-inspired-her-new-album-1.37349

"I don't think I'll ever write a better song than that…", *Cosmopolitan*, December 2011

Seven: Hurts So Good

"I just wanted to make good songs…", www.spin.com, May 28, 2010, http://www.spin.com/articles/exclusive-adele-studio

"to play a few songs and say, 'Hey, I'm back'", Scott Greer, *Billboard*, January 28, 2011, http://www.billboard.com/features/adele-the-billboard-cover-story-1005015182.story#/features/adele-the-billboard-cover-story-1005015182.story?page=3

"I was going to call it 'Rolling In The Deep'…", 89.3 The Current, Minnesota Public Radio, October 21, 2010, http://minnesota.publicradio.org/display/web/2010/10/21/adele-live/

"We want to make sure everywhere is set up perfectly...", Ben Beardsworth interview, *Music Week*, November 15, 2010, http://www.musicweek.com/story.asp?sectioncode=1&storycode=1043294

"I got really upset, actually...", *the gentlewoman*, Spring and Summer 2011

"...luckily it was a wide shot...", Smooth Radio, January 12, 2011, http://www.youtube.com/watch?v=IIDT7skbtt0&feature=autoplay &list=PL6FCA6E096B41DBFC&lf=rellist&playnext=1)

"...the less than revolutionary thought...", review, www.holymoly. com, January 25, 2011, http://www.holymoly.com/reviews/music/ live-review-adele-album-launch-tabernacle-london-2401201152545

"It felt like Whitney Houston meets Obama...", www.dailyrecord. co.uk, January 28, 2011, http://www.dailyrecord.co.uk/showbiz/ music-news/2011/01/28/chart-topper-adele-paris-police-escort-made-me-feel-like-whitney-houston-meets-barack-obama-86908-22881499/

"All day I was thinking, this is gonna be a disaster...", *The Observer*, March 27, 2011

"I thought it was fuckin' shit actually...", Q, July 2011

"Sometimes the stars just align for you...", Jonathan Dickins, *The Observer*, March 27, 2011

"He has no fucking right...", *Rolling Stone*, April 24, 2011

"He gave them private childhood photographs...", Q, July 2011

"I fucking hate being in them...", ibid

"There was a note saying...", www.out.com, http://www2.out. com/features/2011/05/Adele-Lady-Sings-The-Blues/?slideshow_ title=Adele-Lady-Sings-The-Blues&theID=2#Top

"I get a lot of mail from people...", ibid

"I was home, I'm so patriotic...", Q, July 2011

Eight: Little Voice

"I'm not smoking, I'm not drinking alcohol...", people.com, April 5, 2011, http://www.people.com/people/videos/0,,20479173,00.html

"rather my voice be a bit shit…", www.thisislondon.co.uk, June 10, 2011, http://www.thisislondon.co.uk/showbiz/article-23958890-adele-prefers-smoking-to-sound.do

"I had to sit in silence for nine days…", *The Observer*, March 27, 2011

"from the moment Adele stepped out…", review, www.about.com, May 28, 2011, http://top40.about.com/od/concerts/fr/adele-concert-review-denver-colorado-may-2011.htm

"Attending an Adele concert…", review, www.sgn.org, August 12, 2011, http://www.sgn.org/sgnnews39_33/page22.cfm

"Every note was clear and powerful…", review, *Newcastle Journal*, September 17, 2011, http://www.journallive.co.uk/culture-newcastle/music-in-newcastle/2011/09/17/review-adele-at-o2-academy-newcastle-61634-29436885/

The 'Big' Issue

"I don't make music for ears…", *Rolling Stone*, April 28, 2011, http://www.rollingstone.com/music/news/adele-opens-up-about-her-inspirations-looks-and-stage-fright-in-new-rolling-stone-cover-story-20110413

"Who doesn't get airbrushed?…", *The Los Angeles Times*, June 21, 2009, http://articles.latimes.com/2009/jun/21/image/ig-adele21/2

"I've been the same weight since I was 15…", ibid

"The Spice Girls when I was nine…", Q, July 2011

"I hate that idea…", *the gentlewoman*, Spring and Summer, 2011

"I never fell under that spell…", Q, July 2011

"I wouldn't encourage anyone to be unhealthily overweight…", ibid

"I don't have a message…", *Vogue*, October 2011

"Confirmed: Gaga will not be wearing her meat dress…", as reported in the *Daily Mail*, November 14, 2011

Nine: The Secret Of Her Success

"If my record can make somebody be like…", www.salon.com, February 25, 2011, http://www.salon.com/2011/02/25/adele_heartbreak_heroine_gay_icon/

"I want to be making records forever…", *The Guardian*, December 11, 2008

"triumph of anti-marketing…", *The Word*, October 2011

"We knew people had to experience her…", Steve Barnett, *Billboard*, January 28, 2011, http://www.billboard.com/#/features/adele-the-billboard-cover-story-1005015182.story?page=2

"…it's just music, it's just really good music…", Richard Russell, *The Guardian*, May 29, 2011

"I never met her…", *the gentlewoman*, Spring and Summer, 2011

"All of them have put up with a lot of shit…", ibid

"Gay or straight, aged 21 or 65…", www. salon.com, February 25, 2011, http://www.salon.com/2011/02/25/adele_heartbreak_heroine_gay_icon/

"I want people to feel at home when they see me…", *the gentlewoman*, Spring and Summer, 2011

"The key to great singers…", Jonathan Dickins, *Billboard*, January 28, 2011, http://www.billboard.com/#/features/adele-the-billboard-cover-story-1005015182.story?page=2

"It's much easier to try and hide behind a façade…", Paul Epworth, *NME*, May 13, 2011, http://www.nme.com/nme-video/paul-epworth-at-the-great-escape-2011/942847065001

"When she sings, there's just the thinnest veil…", Dan Wilson, Cities97, August 23, 2011

"The New Boring…", *The Guardian*, October 8, 2011

Reality Chick

"The whole idea of being a celebrity…", *The Observer*, March 15, 2009

"I always think I can do better…", 89.3 The Current, Minnesota Public Radio, October 21, 2010, http://minnesota.publicradio.org/display/web/2010/10/21/adele-live/

"It was a bijou flat in West London…", Jo Whiley, *Vogue*, October 2011

"I'm scared of audiences…", *Rolling Stone,* April 28, 2011

"Thing is, the bigger the freakout…", *Vogue*, October 2011

"My nerves don't really settle…", *Observer Music Monthly*, March 15, 2011, http://www.guardian.co.uk/music/video/2009/mar/15/adele-adkins-grammy-tour

"I can't help but talk…", *The Observer*, March 27, 2011

"When I hear artists say…", ibid

"I will not do festivals…", Q, July 2011

"Say the number 18,000 to her…", Jonathan Dickins, *Vogue*, October 2011

"I'm in the worst profession…", *the gentlewoman*, Spring and Summer 2011

"Look at Meryl Streep…", *Vogue*, October 2011

"I got down on my knees and cried…", BBC Radio 1 Live Lounge, January 27, 2011, http://www.bbc.co.uk/programmes/p00dkmnv

"like an actual dream…", Q, February 2011

"I actually heard her piss come out…", *The Graham Norton Show*, April 2011

"My highlights are always stuff in the UK…", ITN Showbiz, December 31, 2008

http://www.youtube.com/watch?v=C08dSExKElk

"Quality control is vital…", *Billboard*, December 9, 2011, http://www.billboard.com/column/the-juice/features/news/adele-artist-of-the-year-q-a-my-career-isn-1005641752.story#/column/the-juice/features/news/adele-artist-of-the-year-q-a-my-career-isn-1005641752.story

"I found it really unnecessary…", Q, July 2011

"I don't want to see me plastered everywhere…", *Vogue*, October 2011

"There's so many people who believe their own hype…", www.out.com, http://www2.out.com/features/2011/05/Adele-Lady-Sings-The-Blues/?slideshow_title=Adele-Lady-Sings-The-Blues&theID=5#Top

"Don't believe the hype…", www.clashmusic.com, January 17, 2011, http://www.clashmusic.com/feature/hometown-hero-adele-interview

"Sometimes I don't know what possesses me to do it…", *Calgary Sun,* March 13, 2011, http://www.calgarysun.com/entertainment/music/2011/03/10/17569906.html

"People start treating you differently…", Q, July 2011

"I'm good with my money…", ibid

"I'll have the final word on everything…", BBC Radio 4, April 3, 2011, http://www.bbc.co.uk/programmes/b00zzmsh

"I wasn't prepared for my success at all…", *Observer Music Monthly,* March 15, 2009

http://www.guardian.co.uk/music/video/2009/mar/15/adele-adkins-grammy-tour

"The more successful I get…", Q, July 2011

"I've been doing this since I was 19…", ibid

"I'm just gonna lay some concrete…", *Billboard*, December 9 2011, http://www.billboard.com/column/the-juice/features/news/adele-artist-of-the-year-q-a-my-career-isn-1005641752.story#/column/the-juice/features/news/adele-artist-of-the-year-q-a-my-career-isn-1005641752.story

"It's been fucking brilliant…", ibid

"When it comes to staying myself…", ibid

"I'm incredibly private…", ibid

Epilogue: When Everyone Cared
"Do the work and make the music…", www.clashmusic.com, January 17, 2011, http://www.clashmusic.com/feature/hometown-hero-adele-interview

"I'm not expecting my next record to be as big as this one…", *NME*, July 4, 2011

http://www.nme.com/news/adele/57747